THE TRADITION OF SCOTTISH PHILOSOPHY

The Tradition of Scottish Philosophy

A New Perspective on the Enlightenment

ALEXANDER BROADIE

First published in Great Britain in 1990 by Polygon

This revised edition first published in 2011 by
John Donald, an imprint of Birlinn Ltd

West Newington House
10 Newington Road
Edinburgh EH9 1QS

www.birlinn.co.uk

ISBN: 978 1 906566 40 1

British Library Cataloguing-in-Publication Data
A catalogue record for this book is available
on request from the British Library

Typeset by Antony Gray
Printed and bound in Britain
by Bell and Bain Ltd, Glasgow

Contents

Acknowledgements

I am grateful to Patricia S. Martin who has provided invaluable assistance checking my assertions biographical and bibliographical and reining back my tendency to rhetorical excess.

A. B.

Glasgow 2011

1 Introduction

The chief aim of this book is to give an account of the philosophical ideas of major figures from two great periods in the history of Scottish culture. One of the periods is the six decades immediately preceeding the Scottish Reformation in 1560. The second period is that of the Scottish Enlightenment, the extraordinary flourishing of high culture which is generally held to have taken place during the greater part of the eighteenth century, perhaps spilling over into the first few years of the nineteenth.[1]

There is universal agreement that from the philosophical point of view Scotland has never mounted a more dazzling display than during the Enlightenment, and it is almost universally agreed that it has never mounted another display which even remotely matches it. An extraordinary group of thinkers dominated the philosophy of the Scottish Enlightenment. The group includes Francis Hutcheson (1694–1746), David Hume (1711–1776), Thomas Reid (1710–1796), Adam Smith (1723–1790), Adam Ferguson (1723–1816) and Dugald Stewart (1753–1828). Their writings are a priceless source of insights into a wide range of perennial, and therefore also of present-day, problems.

I am not at all seeking to belittle the remarkable achievements of the Enlightenment when I say that the very heavy concentration of attention upon that period has led to a seriously distorted picture of the history of Scottish culture in general and the history of Scottish philosophy in particular. In this book I shall try to take a step towards a truer picture. My hope, then, is not that the Enlightenment will have a less good press in the future, but that another great period of achievement in the history of Scottish philosophy will come, in its turn, to secure the attention it has always merited and never received. The other period in question, from around 1500 to 1560, was a time of intense intellectual activity for Scottish academics both in the three home universities – those of St Andrews, Glasgow and King's College, Aberdeen – and furth of Scotland, especially at the University of Paris.[2]

It was not only philosophy that Scottish academics had on their minds at that time. We are speaking here of the religious revolution of which Martin Luther was a partial cause. On the Continent the Reformation was having an increasing effect upon academic life and intellectual life more generally, and Scotland was not immune to the new ideas – indeed, was contributing to them. John Knox, the Reformation's leader in Scotland, referred to a fellow-Scot, John Mair (or Major), as a man 'whose word was then held as an oracle on matters of religion'. Mair was the chief figure in the group of sixteenth-century Scottish philosophers upon whom I shall be focusing in the earlier part of this book. He was a colleague of Erasmus and friend of Cardinal Wolsey. Almost certainly amongst the people who heard Mair lecture during his period as professor at the University of Paris were John Calvin, Ignatius Loyola, François Rabelais and George Buchanan. We are then speaking of a man whose significance was great, in respect of his work both inside this country and abroad.

The earlier flowering of philosophy in Scotland was not however the start of the tradition of philosophy in this country. The first truly great Scottish philosopher was John Duns Scotus (*c*.1266–1308). Duns Scotus came from the village of Duns in the Scottish Borders. His early intellectual development must have been notable, and had there been a university in Scotland at that time he would no doubt have attended it. Instead, when he was about twelve he was taken by two Franciscan friars down to England, where he continued his education at Oxford, became a Franciscan friar, and went on to teach theology at Paris and then, during the last year of his life, at the Franciscan College in Cologne. I used to think that the fact that he left Scotland at the latest in his early teens and did not return, means that it is not appropriate to put him at the start of the history of Scottish philosophy, but am now persuaded that that was an error. It seems always to have been impossible not to identify Scotus with Scotland, for though he was educated in England, taught in France and died in Cologne, he was known throughout ecclesiastical and academic Europe by his country of birth; he was Scotus, the Scot. And this is how his successors in Scotland thought of him. John Ireland (*c.*1440–1495), whom we shall encounter in Chapter 2, quotes Scotus more often than any other medieval writer, and indeed all of Ireland's extant works contain references to him. John Mair is proud to tell us of the physical proximity of his home to Scotus's; Scotus 'was born at Duns, a village eight miles distant from England, and separated from my own home by seven or eight leagues only'.[3] While at Paris Mair published a critical edition of one of the great works of Scotus, the *Reportata Parisiensia*, and repeatedly in his writings Mair refers to Scotus, not by name but as *conterraneus* – my compatriot or fellow-countryman. In important ways the very influential John Mair was himself influenced by Scotus, and his Scotistic interests and tendencies must have been at work during his lectures at Glasgow (where Mair was Principal from 1518 to 1525) and at St Andrews (where he was provost of St Salvator's from 1534 to 1550). Even if Scotus did not attend university in Scotland, or teach here, he was an intimate part of the Scottish tradition of philosophy in virtue of the fact that he was from Scotland, received his pre-university education in Scotland, and was taken up by subsequent Scottish philosophers, for whom his nationality was a source of evident pride. During the decades before the Scottish Reformation it was difficult for Scottish philosophers to philosophise as if there had been no Scotus. It is not however on Scotus himself that I shall be focused in the earlier part of the book, as my attention will be primarily on the writings of a group of Scottish philosophers, the circle of John Mair, who worked two centuries after Scotus; for I wish to demonstrate that philosophy was deeply imbedded in Scottish culture before the Enlightenment, and that the Enlightenment itself, awesome as it was, was not quite as isolated a cultural flourish in Scottish history as it is often made to appear. Scotus was an early voice in an immensely rich philosophical tradition. It is past belief that in the absence of the first four centuries of that tradition the philosophy of the Scottish Enlightenment could have been written.[4]

The earliest teachers in the Scottish universities were graduates of continental universities, rather than English ones, and among continental universities the one then attracting the greatest number of Scottish students was Paris. There they did far more than receive an education; they also stayed to teach others, to write, and to contribute to the administration of the university. Thus for example between its foundation and the Reformation the University of Paris enjoyed the benefits of seventeen or eighteen Scottish rectors. The fact that there were many Scottish academics with a sound grasp of the principles of university administration is of great importance for understanding the origins of the University of St Andrews, for that university was in large measure set up and run by men who had been educated at Paris and had stayed on to teach there. One might almost say that the University of St Andrews was a small version of its alma mater at Paris.[5] The same is true also of the University of Glasgow and of King's College, Aberdeen: all three of them were major centres of philosophical activity in Pre-Reformation Scotland.

For many, at least among those brought up within the Reformed tradition, some of the things said by the Pre-Reformation philosophers may sound strange. One reason is that during the earlier period practically all Scottish philosophers were Catholic priests, as compared with the later when almost all were neither Catholic priests nor even Catholic. Of course, a Catholic priest cannot write from outside his faith. He has a certain concept of the saving truths, and his philosophy will be aimed above all at shedding light upon those truths by showing the extent to which they have a rational basis. This is not to say that a truth is somehow suspect if it cannot be demonstrated. On the contrary some truths which save are mysteries which by their nature are scarcely within the intellectual grasp of humans in this life, and only by a very few were they thought of as capable of demonstration. But if a truth proclaimed by the Church does admit of demonstration then the demonstration should be displayed if only to confirm the faith of the faithful and also to help bring within the fold those whose wavering might perhaps be ended by their being brought to recognise that a given truth has the support of logic. It would be incredible if such an attitude to the truths which save did not affect a philosopher's philosophising.

After the Reformation the old order was replaced and philosophy could not be unaffected. But the sixteenth-century religious revolution had two faces. As well as the more straight-forwardly religious one there was another. Renaissance humanism became the dominant ethos of many, perhaps most, of the universities of Europe. The relations between the Reformation and the humanist movement are numerous, and operate on many levels. One evident relation is the interest in the classical languages, Hebrew, Greek, and Latin. The language of the Universal Church had been Latin, and its Bible was in Latin, though by no means the Latin of the Roman orators, poets, or historians. Hebrew and Greek were the languages of the Old and New Testaments. One reason for the sharply renewed interest in the classical languages was precisely the perceived need for a critical edition of the Bible.

A feature of the educational reform policy in Scotland in the years after the Scottish Reformation, a policy commonly identified with Andrew Melville,[6] was the emphasis placed on the study of Hebrew, though there is evidence of interest in Hebrew in Scottish educational circles decades before Melville's reforms came into effect. Given that lectures on Hebrew were being delivered in the University of Louvain from 1520, and in the University of Paris from 1530, and given the large number of Scottish students at those universities during that period, it is not to be wondered at that an interest in Hebrew was to be found in Scotland.[7] For example, Florence Volusenus (or Wilson) (whom we shall consider in Chapter 7) wrote psalm commentaries in 1531 and 1532 in which he makes reference to the commentaries of Abraham ibn Ezra and David Kimchi. Volusenus is known to have presented George Buchanan with a copy of the Hebrew dictionary by Sebastian Münster (Basle, 1531), and there is evidence that two decades later John Davidson, first Protestant principal of the University of Glasgow, had a serviceable knowledge of Hebrew.

Interest in Greek was stimulated by a desire to establish a critical edition not only of the New Testament, but also of the writings of classical Greece. There was especially a wish to know what Aristotle wrote, for the desire for a fresh start in religious thinking was accompanied by a desire for a fresh start in philosophy, and in each case the plan was to return to universally recognised roots, the Bible and Aristotle. Scotland was as deeply affected by this attitude as was any country in Europe.

Before the Reformation, and indeed at least from the time of St Thomas Aquinas (1224/5–1274), Aristotle had been the central figure in philosophy. But he was studied in Latin translation, and by people with different concerns from those of the humanists. After the Reformation no Scottish philosopher could write on Aristotle as John Mair did in his Commentary (1530) on Aristotle's greatest ethical work, the *Nicomachean*

Ethics. In the dedication to the Commentary (a dedication to his friend Cardinal Wolsey, by then stripped of all his powers) Mair writes: 'In almost all [Aristotle's] opinions he agrees with the Catholic and truest Christian faith in all its integrity . . . in so great and manifold a work, if it be read as we explain it, you meet scarcely a single opinion unworthy of a Christian gentleman.'

Perhaps the most conspicuous act of medieval philosophy was what has been termed the baptism of Aristotle; he was Christianised. The humanists, however, sought the pagan Aristotle, Aristotle in his own person, and that person was a Greek-speaking philosopher from three centuries before the Incarnation. The pagan Aristotle was the one who was discussed in Scottish universities after the Reformation. We shall see, however, that Mair would not have been wholly out of sympathy with the humanist programme. He would have approved of the return to the classical Greek text, and did himself attend classes in Greek. But in this respect he seems to have been an exception among Scottish philosophers of his generation. From the time of Mair's attendance at the Greek classes given in Paris by Girolamo Aleandro, a great deal had to be accomplished to make possible the lectures on Aristotle given by Robert Rollock, first principal of Edinburgh University who, at the end of the sixteenth century, devoted much of his lecture hour to the slow dictation of the original Greek texts.

Perspectives require to be maintained. Whatever the differences between Mair and Rollock, they amount to less than the differences between Rollock and David Hume. Some of the latter differences will be spelled out in due course. Here I should like to say something about the philosophical problems which were addressed by the Pre-Reformation Scottish philosophers. Philosophers ask questions about the nature of existence, and about the kind of existence possessed by what is said to exist; about what knowledge is and what can be known; and about human free will. The questions, and the answers proposed, often seem to be at a very high level of abstraction, and hardly to relate to ordinary human experience, and yet it is just such experience that forces the questions upon us, and often with great urgency.

This is particularly obvious in the case of questions concerning our freedom to act. What is at issue here is not political freedom but metaphysical. The question is not whether our political masters leave us much or little room to do what we want, but whether there are inexorable forces, natural or otherwise, which so constrain us that it is impossible for us to perform any acts other than the ones we do perform. Do we have to say that though we are conscious of ourselves as free, our freedom is illusory, and that we are no freer than heavenly bodies in their courses and plants seeking the sunlight? In that case if we insist that we are free, perhaps we have to say that freedom is a kind of necessity. In attending to the Pre-Reformation Scottish philosophers we shall have a good deal to say about this problem.

A closely related position will also have to be considered. Since God is omniscient there is no human act, past, present, or future, of which He is ignorant. But if God now has total knowledge of some act that I am going to perform at a given time it is surely impossible for me not to perform the act when the time comes for its performance. If God knows that I am going to perform it and yet I do not perform it, then God was in error and therefore is not omniscient. Since He is omniscient I cannot not do what He knows I will, and therefore am not free not to perform it. This argument applies equally to every action by myself or anyone else. Yet not only do we say we have a will; many have held that it is precisely in respect of our possession of a will that we are in the image of God. This is a problem which will concern us in the next chapter, though it can be noted here that modern discussions on how, if at all, our will can be free if nature is a system of universal casual law, match in an uncanny way the various positions adopted by the medieval thinkers in dealing with the question of how, if at all, our will can be free if God is omniscient.

Problems concerning knowledge will occupy a large part of this book. A central question concerns whether we know as much, or even remotely as much, as we think we do. A standard starting point for this question is the fact that some of our experiences of the physical world are illusory. In the light of such experiences we can ask whether there is any sure test of whether or not an experience is true; and if no test is forth-coming, we might start to wonder whether all our experiences of the physical world are illusory, and whether indeed the physical world really exists. This sceptical concern over whether our supposed knowledge of the physical world is really a kind of ignorance precisely parallels the concern articulated earlier over whether our supposedly free acts really are free or whether instead our freedom amounts to no more than a kind of ignorance of the causal determinants of our acts. Perhaps we have to say that the manner of existence of the physical world, the world 'out there', is really no different from that of any object of our imagination. Even if we do not maintain this but argue instead that the external world has a radically different form of existence from that of an object of imagination, a question can be raised concerning how our knowledge of that world is possible. It might be said that it is not difficult for us to grasp how we know an object which is a product of our own imagination, for we created that object; but how can we know something which is sufficiently independent of us to be able, we are certain, to continue existing when we start to think of some-thing else, or even die? As we shall see, major Scottish thinkers dealt with this problem.

The above paragraphs indicate, in a highly schematic fashion, some of the great problems with which we shall be concerned. I shall for the most part be painting with broad sweeps, and covering much philosophical ground. Some of the philosophical discussion in the following pages, particularly those pages devoted to the medieval scene, will make for difficult reading, though I shall try to keep the exposition as simple as possible. However some of the issues are intrinsically both hard and complex, and a determined effort to simplify them will result in something which is not so much a simplification as a falsification. It is important to be as accurate as possible in the details of the exposition partly because much of the important philosophy takes place at the level of detail, even of fine detail; and partly because certain crucial parallels which I wish to demonstrate between the doctrines of the medieval and the Enlightenment philosophers are in those details.

As a first step towards establishing philosophical links between the Pre-Reformation and the Enlightenment periods I shall turn briefly to Lawrence of Lindores, a dominant figure at St Andrews during its first years,[8] its first rector, Paris educated, a teacher at Paris before his return to Scotland, and Scotland's first inquisitor-general. As rector he was well placed to ensure that doctrines he did not like were not taught. The minutes of the Arts Faculty reveal that Lawrence was instrumental in banning the teaching of realism.[9] Here I shall pause to say some words on the concepts, central to philosophy, of realism and nominalism. What I say here will provide a basis for comparison with the Enlightenment and will also shed light on an important feature of the philosophy available to students in Scotland in the early fifteenth century.

Suppose I see two cats, A and B. They are different from each other, for there are two cats, not one. But they are not entirely different, for in respect of being cats they are identical. That is, there is something that A and B both are, namely, a cat. We have here a case of identity in difference. There are things we can say about the kind of existence cats have. They are, at least in part, physical objects, located, as all such objects are, in space and time; and, on a common sense view, they exist independently of any observer. But what should be said about that which the two cats share and in virtue of which we classify them as cats? They have what medieval philosophers called a 'common nature', their 'cathood'. But there are large problems concerning this common nature. For example, we might ask what proportion of the common nature of a cat is in cat A. The obvious answer is that all of it is, for otherwise A would not be completely a cat. If we were to say that part of the common nature, the cathood, is in A and that a different part is in cat B, then A would be only partly a cat and B would be also. But since A must have the whole common nature of a cat, for it is after all a cat and not just partly a cat, then it seems to follow that there can be no more than one cat at a time, for if one cat has the common nature of a cat there is nothing left of that common nature for any other cat to have. This puzzle, one aspect of the territory known as the problem of universals, has prompted a number of solutions. One that is commonly met with is to deny that a common nature is in what has that nature. Those who say that a common nature is in the 'real world out there', and in particular is in the things with that nature, are realists. Their opponents, who say that it is not in the real world out there, are nominalists.

According to the nominalist solution to our puzzle, when we see two resembling objects we form a concept of that in respect of which they resemble. Under this concept we can bring an unlimited number of things – everything which is like the two objects in the relevant respect. According to this view a common nature is not something which exists out there in the real world, but is instead a concept in our mind, a principle of classification which enables us to bring order to our experience of the world. There are several merits to this solution to the problem of universals. One important one is that it resolves the paradox that a realist-type common nature must, as indivisible, exist in only one thing and therefore is not shareable by many things, and therefore is not in fact a common nature at all. The nominalist solution, that the common nature is an indivisible concept in our mind, has the merit of showing how it is possible for infinitely many things to have a common nature. In that case the common nature is indeed common, according to the nominalist account of the matter, in the sense that there is nothing in the common nature that prevents it being common to many things.

This position is itself open to criticism from the realist side. For example, a realist would wish to know what it is about each of many objects that permits all those objects to be brought under the single concept. Surely, he says, it is because they all have something in common that they can be brought under it, and in that case does the nominalist not presuppose the realist position? This is not the place to enter into the details of the debate. Here it is sufficient to note that Lawrence of Lindores, totally committed to the truth of nominalism, had sufficient power, in his role as rector of St Andrews University, to prohibit the teaching of the realism of Albert the Great. His ban was not revoked till the end of his rule.[10]

For the medieval philosophers metaphysical positions always linked up directly with theological ones. The dispute between nominalism and realism was no exception. It is probable that Lawrence of Lindores regarded realism as not merely false but also dangerous, as having a damaging effect upon people's understanding of truths which save. I will give one example of this. A question can be raised concerning the relation between God and norms of justice. God is the God of justice. But that tells us nothing as to whether the norms of justice which structure His acts are dependent upon God or independent of Him. On this matter the realist will take the same sort of line in respect of norms of justice as he takes in respect of common natures. He will say that it is because certain acts are just that God performs them, and that those norms are independent of the divine will. God, like ourselves, is bound by them, even if, as must surely be held, we are of such a nature that we sometimes follow those norms and sometimes do not, whereas God by His nature is constrained to obey them – that is, He obeys them by nature, somewhat as a stone thrown into the air will by nature fall to the ground.

But this doctrine was thought by many to have intolerable consequences, especially because it contradicts the doctrine of the absolute freedom of God. For if the realist is correct on this matter it follows that God's will is, after all, constrained by those norms. God, by an intellectual act grasps the norms and their validity, and then wills in accordance with what he has understood. Of course the nominalist does not wish to say that God is ever unjust. Instead he posits a quite different account of the relation between God and the norms of justice, and a correspondingly different account of the relation between God's intellect and His will. The nominalist solution is to say that those very norms are themselves dependent for their existence upon the divine will. Thus God does not first, with an act of intellect, grasp those norms, and then act on them. He begins by willing the norms into existence. In this sense, though perhaps not in other senses, the moral norms which we regard as absolute and necessary, possess the same sort of radical contingency that everything in the created order possesses. For whatever exists, except God Himself, is, on this view, a product of a divine act of absolutely free will.

Nominalists characteristically placed greater emphasis upon God's will than upon His intellect, and this led them, in general, to become gradually more suspicious of natural theology, roughly the investigation of the created, natural order for clues to the nature of the Creator. For what clues could there be? Let us suppose that God's will is absolutely free, or is constrained only, or at most, by the laws of logic; then we seem forced to the conclusion that though God did indeed create our world He could instead have created an infinitely different world. Hence for any feature in our world which might tempt us to draw a given conclusion about God's nature, a contrary feature would have been present in another world which God could have created instead.

If consideration of the created order does not permit us to draw conclusions about God's nature, to what can we turn for such insight? As a matter of historical fact there was an increasing tendency during the century leading up to the Reformation to turn to the evidence provided by God's revelation of Himself in history. No doubt this was one cause of the humanist pressure towards securing critical texts of the Greek New Testament and of the Hebrew Old Testament. I mention the matter here as providing some evidence not only for the theological significance of the nominalist position but also for the role that the position played in the encroachment of humanist values in the universities during the critical period leading up to the Reformation.

There is no doubt a certain irony in the fact that St Andrews University, which was set up as a bastion of orthodoxy against heresy and 'errors', should itself have played host to some prominent nominalists, including Lawrence of Lindores. I am not for a moment ascribing heretical views to Inquisitor-General Lawrence of Lindores, who was himself directly implicated in the burning of two men for heresy[11]; a doctrine can work itself out in history in a way which would have horrified some who had whole-heartedly embraced that very doctrine. We should not forget, in this context, that St Andrews University was, in due course, to become a centre of Protestant resistance against the forces of the Counter-Reformation. Lawrence would have been mortified.

2 *The Mirror of Wisdom*: Philosophy in the Scots Tongue

Some ten years after the end of Lawrence of Lindores' rule at St Andrews, John Ireland was born, probably in that same town. He is known to students of Scottish literature as the author of the first prose work in Scots, a work which has, despite its quality, received very little attention. John Ireland ought to be better known than he is, and known for more than the one thing on which his reputation is based. To place his work in context I shall begin by saying something about his life.[12]

He first appears in the records of St Andrews University, where he is reported as graduating Bachelor in Arts in 1455. He must have been about fourteen or fifteen, not an uncommon age at that time for an Arts graduate. He remained in St Andrews studying for his Master's degree, but left in 1459 without graduating, after a dispute with the University authorities. Later that year he matriculated in the University of Paris, graduated MA in 1460, and thereupon began teaching there. He was much respected in his new home, rising to become rector briefly in 1469 (to be succeeded by the Scotsman Thomas Kennedy). In 1474 the French King, Louis XI, issued an ordinance condemning nominalist philosophy and banning the use of nominalist writings in the University of Paris.[13] His move was instigated by his confessor the Bishop of Avranche, and was approved by a number of deputies in the three faculties. The ordinance is rather detailed. It approved and authorised the doctrines of Aristotle, Averroes, Albert the Great (who had been especially out of favour with Lawrence of Lindores), Aquinas,

23

Giles of Rome, Alexander of Hales, John Duns Scotus, and Bonaventure; and it rejected the doctrines of Ockham, Buridan, Pierre d' Ailly, Marsilius, and their imitators. The prohibition on teaching those rejected doctrines was accompanied by a threat of banishment against all who disobeyed. The king also required all the masters, present and to come, to swear that they would obey. Meantime the rejected books were to be removed from the University or chained in the libraries to prevent their being borrowed.

The prohibition, which followed similar moves elsewhere, was almost certainly motivated by theological considerations. For the University the prohibition was a serious matter not to be accepted without protest and a deputation was sent to the king to seek its revocation. One member of the deputation was John Ireland, who can be supposed to have approached the task with mixed feelings, since he was after all not even a Frenchman, but a foreign national protesting to the king about the royal action. However, Ireland was one of the more prominent nominalists in the University and there is no surprise in his being chosen for the deputation. We know of his nominalism from his own writings, since he makes his allegiance clear in a number of places. His eloquence was to no avail on that occasion, though the ban was lifted in 1481, and there is some reason to think that Ireland may have been partly responsible for that subsequent royal change of mind, though there is evidence that the King may never have had great enthusiasm for the ban; and in the absence of the Bishop of Avranche rather little effort was required to effect the change to a more balanced curriculum.

By the time of that later revocation Ireland had already returned to Scotland. We do not know the precise date of his return, but on 15 July 1480 he was sitting with the Lords of the Council hearing civil causes. He also sat in Parliament, and was used on several occasions by James III as an ambassador. Ireland was close to James III, becoming his chaplain and confessor. He was a busy man, then, in a variety of fields, which did not however stop him writing a great deal, much of it now lost. But two of his books which are extant are an invaluable source of information about his philosophical and theological ideas. One of those extant works is a Commentary on Books III and IV of the *Sentences of Peter Lombard*, the standard theology manual in universities for several centuries. Here I shall not be dealing with that Commentary. My concern will be instead with *The Meroure of Wyssdome* [*The Mirror of Wisdom*], completed in 1490, about five years before his death.

Ireland had a great deal to say about God's will. He wills. So also do we humans. Creatures inferior to humans do not will; using a common medieval tag Ireland affirms that they are acted upon and do not act [*aguntur et non agunt*].[14] Humans both act and are acted upon; that is, we are both active and passive. God alone acts and is not acted upon; He is pure act. In respect of our possession of a will we are thus placed between God and non-human animals. But our will, though it is that in virtue of which we are in the image of God, enables us to act against our God-given nature as well as in accord with it. Animals cannot do that; they express their nature in all they do. We are by nature rational beings, and yet we can, by will, act against our reason. This, for Ireland, has immediate theological implications. To act against our reason, he tells us, is thereby to commit an offence against God.[15] In a word, it is to sin. In sinning we become worthy of punishment, just as in acting well we become worthy of reward. But bestowal of such recompense for our actions is of course a divine prerogative. This has large implications.

Perhaps the most obvious, and one to which Ireland returns repeatedly, concerns the extent of God's knowledge. How can God recompense justly if He is not in possession of all the facts, not just the externals of the acts but their internal features as well? Thus Ireland adopts the scholastic doctrine that 'the intention with which a person acts is a root of reward and punishment',[16] and God knows that intention, perhaps infinitely better than the agent himself does. At any rate this doctrine accords fully with the teaching on divine omniscience. But Ireland knows that that teaching has its own special difficulties; in particular he was heir to the doctrine of God's immutability. In some way that we can hardly appreciate, He knows what was, is, and will be, without Himself changing as the objects of His knowledge change.

Ireland does not offer us help in grasping this concept. A suggestion I have made elsewhere might help here. The muse can present a poet with a poem in an instant. Suddenly he has it, fully formed in his head. The poem itself has a complex temporal structure, in which we find rallentandos, accelerandos, and other complex temporal formations; and yet all this can occur to the poet in an instant. Likewise, a piece of music can come to a composer in an instant, and here even more obviously, we are dealing with something with a temporal structure. What is being suggested is that God knows the acts of His creatures, and knows indeed all the changes which occur in His creation, in the same kind of single act in which a poet or composer grasps the poem or piece of music. There is a great deal more that can be said about this, but that is perhaps sufficient for our present purpose, which is to focus upon a problem concerning the relation between God's knowledge and human acts.

The starting point for Ireland is the fact that we are required to believe that we are free to obey or to disobey God's law. To believe otherwise, states Ireland, is heresy. Likewise we must believe that through our acts we can be recompensed with either eternal life in heaven or eternal damnation. To which Ireland adds that recompense is not secured solely through our own acts; we still require God's help and grace.[17] (On reaching this point in his exposition, we may particularly regret the loss of one of the works of Ireland, that on *auxilium speciale*, the special act of grace by which our acts become meritorious.) He compares the situation to a person who sees the sun shining outside his house and has only to open the shutter to let the light in; but he will not open it. We cannot blame the shutter for there being no light in the house; of course, says Ireland, we blame the person for not letting in the light. It is, crudely put, his fault.

Nevertheless, as Ireland knows, there are real problems here, and he indicates one at once by referring to some who have wondered how there can be any profit whatsoever in doing good and eschewing evil if God has known from all eternity exactly what we would do and exactly what would in the end become of us.[18] He tells us that this argument comes of 'false and evil imagination', but all the same has sufficient respect for it to deal with it at some length.

He takes seriously the claim that in respect of our will we are in the image of God. If we are free then how much more so must God be? For our freedom, though real, is not unlimited; as part of nature we are bound by the laws of nature, and are therefore not free to jump up to the moon, or to breathe an atmosphere of pure nitrogen and survive, and so on. Perhaps even more basically, from the point of view of metaphysics, we are restricted in our point of view. We are not free to inspect the future as we do the present, for we look out upon the world from now, and can only speculate or conjecture (however intelligently) about the future, just as we look out on the world from here as well as now, and thus can only speculate or con-jecture (however intelligently) about the things which are beyond the scope of our senses in the here and now. Our perspective is therefore infinitely restricted, unlike God's. For He has no here or now, unless we say that His here is everywhere and His now is all time – if indeed we can say even that much, given that God, the creator of the natural order and of the spatio-temporal framework of that order, must be supposed to exist outside, and independently of, that framework.

The absolute freedom of God is basic for Ireland. He argues

that its denial leads straight to absurdity. For let us suppose that whatever God creates He creates not freely but by necessity. In that case, argues Ireland, all the products of His creative acts (including ourselves) exist eternally. If created things are created by necessity, their existence is a necessary consequence of God's existence; that is, He only has to exist for the created things to exist. Hence if He exists eternally His creatures also must exist eternally. This is a manifest absurdity. We must conclude, holds Ireland, that God's creative acts are absolutely free. Except on that assumption it is inexplicable how things can exist in time.

Not only are all past creatures created by an absolutely free act of God, so also are all creatures yet to exist. Yet God knows from all eternity exactly what will exist. Is the fact that God is prescient not incompatible with the claim that those creatures will be produced freely? If God always knew they would exist how could it ever be true, right up to the time of their creation, that they would not exist? And in that case is their existence, when it comes, not necessary? Ireland's response to this is to point out that the reason God knew from all eternity that the creatures would exist is that He knew from all eternity that He would freely produce them.[19] His prescience does not necessitate either Him or them. For He was absolutely free not to create those creatures. If, freely, He does not create them, then He knew from all eternity that they would not exist; likewise if, freely, He does create them, then He knew from all eternity that they would exist. Divine prescience, therefore, is compatible with divine freedom to create.

Ireland supports this position with a characteristic piece of scholastic logic. He argues that a proposition's actually being true is compatible with its possibly being false. The proposition which he offers as an example is 'The Day of Judgement will come', which, as an act of faith, he accepts as true. Yet at the same time he accepts the possibility of the proposition's being false, for it is by an absolutely free act of God that the Day of

Judgement will come, and since that act is free, it is open to God not to perform it, in which case of course the Day will not come. Thus, though it is an article of faith that the Day will come, that Day has the metaphysical status of a merely contingent event for it is a product of a free act, and hence the possibility of its non-existence remains with it even while it exists.

The point might also be put, again following Ireland, in this way: If God knows that the Day of Judgement will come, then it will indeed come. That truth is a necessary truth, but it does not follow that either the premiss or the conclusion is necessary. Indeed, as Ireland affirms, the conclusion is contingent, that is, it has the possibility of being either true or false. And its contingency is due to the fact that whether there is a Day of Judgement or not depends on God's free will. But if the conclusion of the inference is contingent then so also, as a matter of logic, the premiss, viz, that God knows that the Day of Judgement will come, is not necessary. And, once again, the reason that that premiss is contingent is that what God knows depends upon what is true, and what is true depends upon what God, by an absolutely free act, brings about.

We might still wonder, however, whether there is any room in this system for the freedom of any acts which are not God's. My acts, after all, are supposed to be mine and not God's. Even if God's prescience is compatible with the possibility of His future creatures not coming into existence, can it not be argued that His prescience is incompatible with my supposedly future free acts not being performed? And if they cannot not be performed then they are necessarily performed, in which case they are not free acts at all. This deep issue in the philosophy of religion is resolved by Ireland along essentially Thomist lines; that solution is perhaps still the most widely canvassed solution to the problem. It starts by a consideration of the relation between human knowledge and its object. Suppose I see a man writing a letter. I am certain that he is writing a letter, since I am looking at him performing the act. But the fact that I have overwhelming perceptual evidence that he is performing the act does not imply that what I know is itself necessary; that is, my knowledge does not necessitate its object. Since I can see the man writing a letter then necessarily he is writing a letter. But the necessity here is not the necessity of the man's act of writing a letter. On the contrary, it is the necessity of the inference 'Since I see him writing a letter he is writing one'. Because it is the inference that is necessary and not the act, I can say that the act is free, despite my certain knowledge of it.[20]

This same point can be made in respect of God's view of human acts. If, from all eternity, He sees a person perform an act, then necessarily that person will perform the act. But what is necessary here is not the act but the inference. What is being said is this: Necessarily if God sees a person perform a given future act then the person will perform it. But the act itself is not any the less free for God's knowing that it will be performed, just as the act is not the less free for our knowing, because we can see it, that it is now being performed. This is Ireland's view.

Underlying this position is the theological point that it is incorrect to speak about God in temporal terms. Admittedly it is difficult for us not to do so, for our verb system is tensed. But that is simply to say that our language is an inadequate instrument for talking about God. In particular, while it is appropriate for us to speak about an act which lies in the future in relation to ourselves, it is not appropriate to speak about an act which lies in the future in relation to God. What we refer to as God's 'prescience' i.e. foreknowledge, is His knowledge of what is present to Him, for what is future in relation to us is present to God; it is as immediate to the divine gaze as any object at which we are now looking is immediate to ours. That is why I spoke earlier of God's 'now' being all time.

Let us return to a question posed earlier concerning God's free will. Ireland invokes the classical theological distinction between predestination and reprobation. For God to predestine a person is for Him to have the purpose of giving that person eternal life in joy, and for God to reprove a person is for Him to have the purpose of withholding from the person eternal life in joy, and of giving him eternal life in pain. Ireland asks whether God predestines and reproves freely, that is, without cause, or whether He is caused to predestine and reprove by the actions of His creatures. There is a dilemma here which Ireland wishes to address. On the one hand there are grounds for saying that the act of predestining or reproving is absolutely free, for all of God's acts are absolutely free. But on the other hand, as Ireland points out, if God predestines and reproves freely, and is not caused to do so by the behaviour of His creatures, then this has strange consequences. In many cases it would seem that a great favour or a great cruelty has been done, for surely it would mean that many who have persevered in sin will have an eternity of joy, and many who have persevered in righteousness will have an eternity of pain.

In response to this argument Ireland insists on the point that God's actions are indeed absolutely free. No creature, by being righteous, forces God's hand. If a person lives a life of righteousness God will, as those with faith affirm, ordain an eternal life of joy for him, and if a person perseveres in sin God will ordain an eternal life of pain for him. But in each case God does so by a free act. He could withhold from each of us what we have come to regard as a just recompense, but He chooses to recompense according to desert. This is something that the faithful affirm as an act of faith.

Nevertheless Ireland has regard for the fact that we do tend to speak in causal terms, that is to say, to see our acts as causally determining God to respond in certain systematic ways, in particular by rewarding the righteous and punishing the sinful. But there is room here for an important scholastic distinction, and Ireland duly makes it. For there are two kinds of cause. First there is a cause of being or existence, and secondly a cause of knowing. God is a cause of being in so far as He creates His creatures, and a human is a cause of being in so far as he produces an artifact. As regards this kind of cause, it is absolutely impossible for any creature to cause anything in God.

The cause of knowing is a quite different matter. There are many things which we know because we see that they follow from other things which we know. What is at issue here is the relation between premiss and conclusion in an inference which is perceived to be valid. I see that proposition Q follows from proposition P, and since I know that P is true I conclude that Q is true also, and I thereupon claim knowledge of Q. Now if I accept, as a matter of faith, that God will recompense people according to their deserts, and I know that a given person has lived a life of righteousness, I may claim to know that God will reward that person with a life of eternity in joy. And there is a kind of causality here from creature to Creator, but the cause in question here is not a cause of being but a cause of knowing. My knowledge of the creature causes in me knowledge of God. And this does not in the least imply that the righteous person has forced God's hand. In so far as anyone is forced into anything, it is me, forced to accept the conclusion in the light of my acceptance of the premiss.

In *The Mirror of Wisdom* John Ireland makes numerous interesting points concerning the relation between God's will and our freedom. I have not mentioned all, or even very many of those points here. And in *The Mirror* he reports that in his Commentary on Book I of the *Sentences of Peter Lombard* he has things to say on God's prescience. The latter book is now, sadly, lost, and we can make only an educated guess as to its contents. But I hope I have said enough to show that *The Mirror* itself is well worth studying for the sake of the insights it affords on this important matter.

3   The Circle of John Mair

Towards the end of John Ireland's stay at the University of Paris a young Aberdonian named James Liddell [Jacobus Ledelh] joined the large number of Scots already there. Liddell took his Master's degree in 1483 and in the following year began teaching at Paris.[21] In 1486 he was appointed examiner of Scottish students there. It is not known whether Ireland knew Liddell, but it is very likely that they met. Such a meeting would have had a symbolic significance for Scottish culture. In 1495 Liddell became the first Scot who, while yet alive, had a book of his printed. Other writings by Scots, in particular by John Duns Scotus, had been printed earlier but Duns Scotus had been dead for over a century and a half when his books were first printed.

Liddell's book is of particular significance for us since it was a philosophical work entitled *Tractatus conceptuum et signorum* [*A Treatise on Concepts and Signs*].[22] It deals with issues relating to the nature of knowledge, and was a forerunner of a number of books by Scots dealing, though at much greater length, with precisely the questions raised by Liddell. The central concept in those treatises was that of a 'notion'. In the next chapter I shall speak in some detail about those Scottish writings on notions, but considerations of politeness dictate that first I introduce the authors in question. I shall say something here about them and their chief Scottish associates.

Some years before Liddell's book appeared there arrived in Paris a remarkable man, John Mair (or 'Major') from the village of Gleghornie near Haddington.[23] He was born *c.* 1467 and attended school at Haddington: 'the town which fostered the beginnings of my studies, and in whose kindly embrace I was nourished as a novice with the sweetest milk of the art of grammar' – Latin grammar, of course, the international language of scholarship, and the language in which he wrote all of his very many books. For, unlike Ireland, Mair appears never to have used his native tongue as a means of propagating his ideas. His movements after leaving grammar school are unclear. It has been speculated that he was a student at St Andrews University, but in his Commentary on the *Sentences of Peter Lombard*, written while he was in Paris, he reports that he had never seen the city of St Andrews.[24] That seems conclusive evidence against the speculation. In the preface to his last book, a Commentary on the *Nicomachean Ethics* of Aristotle, Mair tells us that in 1491 he attended Godshouse (in 1505 to be renamed 'Christ's College') in Cambridge, a very unusual choice of university for a Scot at that time, and after a year matriculated at the University of Paris, studying under Jean Bouillache at the College of Sainte-Barbe. He took his Master's degree in 1494, and became regent (that is, lecturer) in Arts in the following year. Meantime he began the study of theology, under Jan Standonck at the College of Montaigu.

Within a very short time he became established as a leading figure at Montaigu. Its teaching staff already included another Haddington man, Robert Walterston, whose regard for his home town is reflected in the fact that he was granted a charter of lands in Haddington to support a chaplain at the local Church of the Holy Trinity. The college played host about that time to an extraordinary group of men including Erasmus, and later including Ignatius Loyola. It is very probable that a large number of the most important people responsible for the religious and humanist changes of the earlier part of the sixteenth century went to hear Mair lecture at Paris. There is certainly eyewitness evidence that he was a compelling lecturer. His writings were criticised by some for their dry 'Sorbonnic' style, but the lecture style of the man was evidently a very different matter.

In 1506 Mair was awarded a doctorate of theology by Paris, by which time he had already published a number of books on logic and philosophy and had acquired a considerable reputation as a teacher and as the leader of a research team. Antonio Coronel, one of his Spanish colleagues and teacher of Calvin, referred to him as 'prince of philosophers and theologians' at the University of Paris, and he was regarded with awe in several quarters. There were a number of Spanish philosopher theologians who were close to Mair during this period, and the story of his 'Spanish circle' is an interesting one yet to be written.[25] I shall be concerned here with his Scottish associates.

In 1518 Mair returned to Scotland. Some years earlier in his Commentary on the fourth book of the *Sentences of Peter Lombard* Mair had written: 'Our native soil attracts us with a secret and inexpressible sweetness and does not permit us to forget it'. The Commentary was dedicated to Alexander Stewart, son of James IV and a pupil of Mair's colleague Erasmus; he died at Flodden, as did other associates of Mair. In 1517 Gavin Douglas, Bishop of Dunkeld and one of Scotland's greatest poets, who some time before had been sent to France to seek to persuade Mair to return to Scotland (with an offer of the treasurership of the Chapel Royal at Stirling), was again in France, this time to play a role in the negotiations which preceded the reaffirmation, in the Treaty of Rouen, of the Auld Alliance. It is possible that on this trip too he sought to persuade Mair to return. Whether Gavin Douglas did indeed play a part in Mair's decision is not certain, though it is probable. In any case, at about this time some negotiations with Mair must have taken place, for in 1518 he took up the post of Principal of the University of Glasgow.

Immediately upon his arrival in Glasgow (which was so far as we know his first visit to the city) he published his Commentary on the Gospel of Matthew, declaring it to have come from the 'Academy of Glasgow' and expressing the hope that that Academy would emulate the Academy of Athens. He remained

Principal for five years, finding time, despite his administrative commitments, to teach both arts and theology. He also found time to write. In 1521 his *Historia Maioris Britanniae [The History of Greater Britain]* was published. The 'Greater Britain' in question is the united kingdom of Scotland and England; for Mair argued that Scotland's future strength lay, not in a continuation of the Auld Alliance, but in a unification with the auld enemie. The printing of the book was the occasion for a brief return by Mair to France for he wished to see the book through the presses. No doubt he would have been glad to have been able to hand the manuscript to a Scottish printer, but it is an important fact about the constraints upon Scottish academic life at that time that there was then no printer in the country who had the technical competence to produce such a large book. It should be added that the book's sales prospects were far better in Paris than in any of the three Pre-Reformation Scottish university towns, since Paris University then had a larger population than had the three medieval Scottish universities combined.

Mair was undoubtedly the most distinguished Principal Glasgow had during the Pre-Reformation period, and also its most renowned teacher.[26] The students at the University were then being taught by perhaps the most formidable arguer in Europe, and a man whose reputation was Europe-wide. For example, in 1522 Domingo de San Juan affirmed that in Salamanca: 'in this flourishing university it was solemnly decreed, and that to no little common advantage and utility of the students, that the nominalist regents in arts should be compelled in the first year of their course to lecture on the dialectic of the revered master John Mair, a man celebrated the world over'.

In 1523 Mair transferred to the University of St Andrews, where he was, till 1525, assessor to the dean of the Arts Faculty. One of his theology students during that period was George Buchanan. On relinquishing that post he returned to Paris, but was back in St Andrews in 1531, becoming in due course the provost of St Salvator's College, a post he occupied till his death, aged about eighty three, in 1550. We do not know where he was buried but the likelihood is that, as had happened in the case of other provosts of the College, he was laid to rest in St Salvator's. Among Mair's many students during his second period at St Andrews was John Knox, who wrote of his teacher that he was a man 'whose word was then held as an oracle on matters of religion'.[27]

One student, and then colleague, of Mair's at the College of Montaigu was David Cranston, a priest of the Glasgow diocese, who died tragically young in 1512, after writing a number of books on logic and philosophy. All his known works are extant, and I shall be discussing one of them, his treatise on notions, shortly.

A pupil of Cranston's, as well as of Mair's, at Montaigu was George Lokert of Ayr.[28] He was born *c.* 1485, and matriculated at Paris in his mid-teens. He became Master of Arts in 1505, and began teaching Arts subjects. In 1519 he became prior of the College of Sorbonne, the headquarters of the Faculty of Theology in the University of Paris, and the following year gained his doctorate in theology. By this time he had written a number of books on logical and philosophical topics as well as preparing an edition of writings by earlier masters on physics. He had already given at least one full course of three and a half years on the *Sentences of Peter Lombard*. If he published that course in the form of a commentary then the commentary has not survived, nor do we have any account of what he said in his theology course. In view of the very high quality of his logical and philosophical writings, this gap in our knowledge of him is particularly a cause for regret.

In 1521 he returned to Scotland, taking up the post of provost of the Collegiate Church of Crichton some miles south of Edinburgh, and, in 1522, the post of rector of the University of

St Andrews, where for two years his colleague and former teacher John Mair was under his jurisdiction. During their occupancy of posts at St Andrews Lokert and Mair made a number of changes in the examinations procedures at St Andrews; changes, not surprisingly, along the lines of reforms recently implemented in Paris. By 1526 Lokert was back in Paris, resuming his fellowship of the College of Sorbonne and becoming also 'overseer' of the Scots College.

He returned to Scotland in the early 1530s, taking up the post of archdeacon of Teviotdale, and then in 1534 becoming dean of Glasgow, a position he held (along with his provostship of Crichton Collegiate Church) till his death in 1547. There is evidence that during this period Lokert was a prime mover in a plan to establish in Glasgow University a college for all the faculties but it came to nothing.[29] No doubt Lokert was involved in a number of ways with the University, but he would in any case have been kept fully occupied as dean of Glasgow; everything we know about Lokert reveals him to have been an indefatigable worker on behalf of the things he identified as good.

The Obit Book of the Church of St John the Baptist in Ayr records that in 1542 he gave instructions for a mass for his late parents to be said in the church; and on his death a mass was said there for the soul of George Lokert also. The probability is that he was buried in Glasgow Cathedral, but no record survives on this matter.

Another Scottish philosopher who should be mentioned here is William Manderston. He was born *c.* 1485 in the diocese of St Andrews, possibly in Haddington, and in 1503 matriculated at the University of Glasgow, an unusual choice for an east-coast man. He received his Bachelor's degree in 1506, and then transferred to the University of Paris where he worked first under, and then as a colleague of, John Mair. His first major publication, which appeared in 1517, was a three-volume work on formal logic. The following year he published a treatise on ethics, to which I shall attend in Chapter 6, and in 1522 his last extant work appeared, dealing with a number of philosophical problems relating to the ascription of truth or falsity to propositions concerning future human acts.

In 1525 Manderston was elected rector of the University of Paris. Shortly after this George Buchanan became his attendant. Something of the esteem in which Manderston was held at this time emerges from a comment written by the procurator of the 'German Nation' at Paris (that being the 'Nation' to which Scots at the University were assigned for administrative purposes): 'Finally we went to the Church of St Julien [a University church near Notre Dame] where Master William Manderston was elected, whose eminent virtue and distinguished erudition in the disciplines of thought have saved the 'German Nation' from the stains and calumny of sterility . . . on the third day also, the deputies of all the faculties gave the greatest thanks to the electors for having chosen such a great man'.

He left Paris early in 1528, and two years later was elected rector of the University of St Andrews. In 1531 he was joined in St Andrews by Mair, who thus had the distinction of serving in St Andrews under the rectorship of two of his former pupils. The rectorship of course was an administrative post, but it did not mark the end of Manderston's work as a teacher, for in 1536 he is described as a lecturer *in actu*, that is, he was delivering lectures. Two years later he was granted tax exemption in view of his work for the common good of the university. That work continued. In 1540 he and Mair jointly founded a bursary in theology and in 1546 Manderston founded a bursary in Arts. He died in 1552. On the 16 May of that year arrangements were made for services for his soul in the parish church of Cupar, Fife.[30]

A further member of Mair's circle is Robert Galbraith (born *c.* 1483) who, in 1505, was responsible, along with David Cranston and George Lokert, for the publication of the collected logic works of Mair. Galbraith rose to become professor of Roman Law at Paris before returning to Scotland to take up a position as senator at the College of Justice in Edinburgh. There is just one extant work by him, a massive four-part investigation of formal logic, one of the great classics of medieval logic. His murder in a family feud in 1544 robbed Scotland of one of its most distinguished scholars.

Liddell was not the only important Scottish thinker of this period to have had close links with Aberdeen. Two others, both associates of Mair, should here be mentioned. One was Gilbert Crab (*c.*1482–1522) who matriculated at the University of Paris at about the time that Cranston started teaching at Montaigu. He published a Commentary on Aristotle's *Politics* while yet an undergraduate and went on to write a number of other works covering ethics, logic, and the theory of knowledge. All these works repay close study. And finally mention must be made of Hector Boece, who rose to become Principal of the recently founded King's College, Aberdeen. A Dundee man, he attended the University of Paris. Boece, like Mair, wrote a history of Scotland, though there is now general agreement that Boece's approach was far less scholarly than Mair's. He also wrote a book on logic which has many interesting things to say on the nature of inference.

I am speaking here of a period in which Scottish students were to be found in universities across Europe, in Vienna, Cologne, Louvain, Bologna, Poitiers, and many others. Here I am concerned with those who were associated with John Mair at Paris, who mastered their craft there, and then, in most cases, returned to enhance the cultural life of their homeland. It is impossible here to go into detail about the many areas of logic and philosophy illuminated by that galaxy of philosophical talent. I shall restrict myself to a discussion of their ideas on two topics, the first dealing with the nature of knowledge, and the second with human freedom.

4 Knowledge

Mair and members of his circle paid close attention to language. They spoke routinely of three kinds of language, spoken, written, and mental.[31] A spoken proposition is any proposition which we are aware of by our sense of hearing. A written proposition is any we are aware of by the sense of sight. David Cranston points out that in this technical sense the nods and other gestures by which a religious under a vow of silence makes known his thoughts are also to be counted as written language; the fact that we see the gestures is sufficient for that classification. A question was duly raised whether we can speak about other kinds of language on the basis of the other sensory receptors. For example, Lokert suggests that a language of smells is possible.[32] And in our own time a tactile language, Braille, is in common use. But speech and writing were undoubtedly the commonest means of communication, and no doubt for that reason special attention was paid to them rather than the more exotic forms of language which, though recognised as theoretical possibilities, hardly if at all impinged upon the daily lives of most people.

Of these two sorts of language the spoken variety was regarded as having a natural priority; we learn to speak before we learn to write. An aspect of this point is that we speak in order that we may communicate our thoughts to those who are present to us, and write in order to communicate our thoughts to those who are absent.[33] Whether right or not, the point is not of great philosophical significance since it depends mainly upon certain facts about us which from the philosophical point of view are unimportant. It would be easy to imagine a community of deaf people for whom written language, that is, a language of nods and other gestures, has priority, and spoken language plays very little part in their communicative acts because of the hearing difficulties shared by the members of the community.

The third type of language I mentioned is 'mental language'. This played a crucially important role in the writings of the members of Mair's circle. A simple spoken proposition can be seen as having a number of parts. For example, 'Fido is brown' has three parts, for in this proposition two terms, 'Fido' and 'brown' are linked by a third 'is' which acts as a *copula*, a kind of coupling device. The proposition represents something, a thought, for when we say 'Fido is brown' we are normally taken to have in our head a notion of Fido, a notion of brown, and a notion of a certain link between them which I express by 'is'. Thus not only does the written proposition have three parts, so also does the thought, and each part of the thought matches a distinct part of the written proposition. In the light of considerations such as these, considerations, that is, about the extent to which we can speak about our thoughts in much the same way that we can speak about our spoken or written language, it was held that thinking itself is done in a kind of language – mental language.

But what language is mental language? Is it English, or French, or Latin, or something else? Perhaps the obvious reply is that it is the same as the spoken language of the speaker, so that if my mother tongue is English my thoughts are in English. Or perhaps we should add that if I am saying my thoughts aloud then the language of my thoughts is the same as the language of the spoken sentences, whatever my mother tongue might be. These, though obvious suggestions, are far from the opinions of our late medieval philosophers. The position presented by Cranston and others, following an Augustinian tradition, is that the language of thought is different from all conventional languages, and makes conventional languages possible. I can express my thought that Fido is brown, in a number of conventional languages. And the thought that Fido is brown, which I duly express in English, is exactly the same as the thought that I duly express in French, and then in Spanish, and so on. The thought, then, is no different for being expressed in all those other languages. The crucial point in the view of Cranston is that one should not suppose that because I express a thought in a given language I must have thought it in that same language. On the contrary, the language of thought is a language of nature which I must possess if it is to be possible for me to have any conventional language.

For example, I look at a tree and in so doing form a concept or notion of the tree; put in ordinary terms, I have an idea of the tree in my mind. Likewise I see the leaves on the tree, and in doing so form a concept or notion of the leaves. I must be capable of forming such notions before I can learn the signification of the spoken or written terms 'tree' and 'leaves'. Certainly if I have no notion of a tree or of leaves, I cannot learn the signification of those two terms. My mental language is composed of such notions, somewhat as English is composed of terms like 'tree' and 'leaves'.

Notions then, the building blocks of mental language, must be distinguished from the conventional expression of them in English, Latin and so on, by the fact that notions have a natural priority over conventional terms. But that is by no means the only difference. We might ask how the notion corresponding to a given English term is spelled. I have a notion of a man and wish to spell the notion. It should be pointed out first that it cannot be spelled the way that the corresponding conventional term is spelled. For which conventional term is at issue? I can spell 'man', which expresses the notion, but what of 'homme' which equally expresses the notion, or 'hombre' or 'anthropos'? We are here at an important metaphysical point in the philosophical considerations about language. Cranston developed the point with particular clarity. We can distinguish between on the one hand the letters which compose a term, and on the other the signification of that term. The letters and the signification are related to the term in totally different ways. The letters can get along nicely without human beings, but the signification is a product of a human act. That is to say, 'man' has a certain signification because we have given it one. The signification might seem to be a quality of the term and in a way it is, but it is more accurate to class it as the mental act by which we understand the term in the way we do. To speak about the signification of a term is to speak about our way of understanding it. On this interpretation, signification is a mental act. The word is in the world, but its signification is in the mind of the reader or listener. This act of understanding (this being Mair's phrase – *actus intelligendi*)[34] is what was termed a notion or mental term; and it is plain that it does not make sense to ask how a notion is spelled, for acts of understanding are not the kind of thing that can be spelled.

A corollary of this is that a mental term or notion cannot change its signification for there is nothing to change. A written term can change its signification for we can decide to give it a new sense; in medieval terminology, we would 'impose a new signification' upon the string of letters and similarly we can impose a new signification on a sound. But since a mental term or notion is not composed of a string of letters or of a sound no new signification can be imposed upon it. Indeed there is nothing whatever to a mental term beyond its signification. There is no 'it' there which is a mental term and which can have first one signification and then another. To think otherwise is to employ the wrong metaphysical categories. It is to think of a mental term as a kind of physical object, when it has to be classed as an act of mind.

In the light of points noted in chapter one when discussing Lawrence of Lindores, it should be plain that we are dealing here with a nominalist theory of meaning, one which places the whole weight upon the dependency of meaning on acts of mind.

Some have held, and some now hold, a realist theory of meaning. According to one major version of realism, now current, which is due to Gottlob Frege, the sense of an expression can have a life of its own independent of the expression which has that sense, and even independent of the temporal world in which the expression exists. Cranston's account of the mode of existence of signification is perhaps as far from the Fregean realist account of sense as it is possible to be. Not only is signification, in Cranston's view, entirely mind dependent, it is also essentially temporal. For there is signification only while there is thinking, and thinking is a temporal act.

Before leaving the topic of mental language, I should like to make a further point. The members of Mair's circle were all logicians first and foremost, and had an especial interest in the formulation of rules of sound argument, that is, rules which enable us to argue in such a way that if our premises are true, then so also must be the conclusion. The sample arguments they presented in their textbooks were in Latin, but the Latin was often unidiomatic and sometimes as far removed from the elegant style of the humanists as anything could be. The reason for this is that the logicians were trying to forge a 'scientific' Latin in which things could be said with the utmost clarity, and in particular with the minimum of ambiguity. They recognised that very often our thinking was a good deal clearer than the overt expression of it, and they sought to match our spoken or written language as closely as possible to our mental language. Mental language came to be seen as a kind of perfect language of which all conventional languages are at best imperfect representatives, and the logicians came to think that one of their chief tasks was to show how mental propositions could be expressed in speech or writing in such a way that the grammatical structure of the utterance and the inscription conformed as closely as possible to the logical structure of the mental propositions which the spoken and written ones expressed.

Mental terms, or notions, were said to be either categorematic or syncategorematic. The terminology is not inviting, but the distinction is perhaps the most important one in the whole of logic, and I should like here to give a brief exposition of the distinction and then to make some philosophical comments about it.

Cranston defines 'notion' in this way: 'A notion is a quality through which a cognitive power knows something. For example, the seeing by which I see a wall is called a notion, because through that seeing, the mind knows the wall.'[35] Gilbert Crab gives much the same definition, while adding a phrase (namely, 'vitally changing the cognitive power') to indicate that what Cranston calls a 'quality' should actually be understood as an act of mind.[36] Both philosophers agree that a notion is of some thing, or of some things. According to this view, given any notion I have, I ought in principle to be able to point to something and say truly that the notion is a notion of that thing. Such a notion is categorematic. Any notion X such that I can point to something and say truly 'That is an X' is categorematic. But George Lokert adds in his definition of 'notion' that it is a quality which immediately represents something or *in some way* to a cognitive power.[37] What is at issue here is whether there are notions corresponding to terms such as 'and', 'or', 'if', 'every', 'some', 'no', and 'is', that is, precisely the terms in which logicians were particularly interested. Certainly one cannot point to something and say meaningfully 'That is an every' or 'That is an or'. Those two propositions are not even grammatically well formed. But the prevalent view was that those terms, though they do not represent any thing, do represent in some way, and as such there can be notions corresponding to them for notions can represent in some way. In what way? Well, if I think that every dog is gentle, I am thinking about dogs and gentleness. But I am doing more than that, for I am also thinking about dogs in a certain way, namely, universally, and I am also thinking unitively, for I am holding together in my mind in a conceptual unity my thoughts of all dogs and of gentleness. Notions which signify not something but in some way, are syncategorematic.

The point just made has an immediate bearing on matters close to the heart of modern linguists and logicians. What is at issue here is what is now spoken of as the order of the construction of propositions. Lokert, typical of the logicians among whom he worked, held that in a proposition such as 'Every dog is gentle' there is a clearly determinable order of construction. I cannot think unitively without thinking unitively about something, so there must already be at least two things in place if I am to think unitively, and hence the proposition is not formed by first thinking 'is' and then adding the rest. I must first be thinking about dogs and gentleness. Furthermore, I cannot think universally without thinking universally about something. Thus I already have to be thinking about dogs if I am to think universally about them. Hence the order of construction of this mental proposition is this: the notions of dogs and gentleness must first be in place, then I think universally about dogs, and finally I think unitively about all dogs and gentleness. This way of looking at the matter bears a striking resemblance to some modern theories.

There is no doubt that amongst our philosophers the key concept in their investigation of the nature of knowledge was that of a 'notion'. However, notions were recognised as being similar to certain other kinds of entities from which it was important to distinguish them. One kind of entity in particular attracted attention, namely, species. Some words about species are therefore in order here.

It was held by several of our philosophers that when perception occurs there are species in the mind, and these species are mental qualities which play a vital role in the perceptual act. In that respect species are certainly similar to notions. But the differences are no less conspicuous, as will become clear if we consider the role species were held to play in our perception of the physical world. Almost from the start philosophers have been interested in sense perception. One problem is how sense perception is possible. This resolves itself into a number of distinct problems, one concerning the fact that perception appears to require action at a distance, that is, it appears to require that one thing acts upon another which is distant from it. How is it possible for something to be miles from me and yet for me to see it? In fact, that the distance in question is great does not add to the difficulty, for once it is supposed that the phenomenon of action at a distance is mysterious, then action upon something six inches away is no less mysterious than is action upon something fifty miles away. If I see something a mile away, then my mind somehow manages to bridge that gap between myself and the object; or, if that presumes too much, the object manages to bridge the gap between itself and me. We should not assume that a similar problem can be raised concerning all the sensory modalities. For me to taste food the object should be contiguous with the sense receptor, and apparently the same thing should be said for touch also. Sound and smell are more problematic. But sight does seem a clear case of action at a distance, and it was most especially in connection with sight that species were introduced into philosophy. According to one account inherited from ancient philosophy, species are miniature replicas of an object which are forever emanating from the object. When these replicas strike a suitably formed sensory receptor, and thence enter the mind, perception occurs.

For those dubious of the possibility of action at a distance this account of species has an obvious advantage, for it allows one to say that perception is not after all a case of action at a distance, for the immediate cause of perception is not the distant object but the species which emanate from it and strike the sensory receptor. The distant object is thus only the mediate cause of perception. In discussing this matter a distinction was sometimes drawn between two kinds of contact, namely, mathematical and virtual. Two objects are in mathematical contact when they are so close to each other that it is not possible for a body to be placed between them. Two objects are in virtual contact when one of them is so present to the other that it has an effect on the other even though the two are not in mathematical contact. Virtual contact, then, involves by definition the exercise of causal power whereas mathematical contact does not. It was William Ockham's view that for an agent to have an effect on something it was not necessary for the agent to be in mathematical contact with it. Ockham's view on this matter was well known. Lokert considers two cases which appear to bear out Ockham's doctrine.[38] First is the case of the magnet which attracts a distant piece of iron without apparently having an effect on the intervening space, and secondly there is the torpedo fish. This makes the fisherman's hand tremble when he holds the net containing the fish, though apparently it does not have an effect on the net itself. Lokert seems uncertain about how to deal with these two cases of action at a distance. Perhaps the magnet does after all have an effect on the intervening space, though of course it does not affect the space in the way in which it affects the iron. And likewise the torpedo fish may have some effect upon the net even if it does not make the net tremble.

Our philosophers were not happy about the idea of action at a distance, if such action is taken to involve an object A affecting a distant object B without affecting it by affecting an intermediate object which itself is the immediate cause of A's alleged effect on B. The problem, in the case of perception, is that, as Lokert points out, species are not themselves available for inspection by the senses. We cannot see them radiating from a visible object. All we can see is the object itself. Species play, therefore, a merely explanatory role in the context of a scientific theory. The success or failure of the hypothesis that species exist, is to be measured in terms of the extent to which the assumption that they exist does in fact explain what they were intended to explain. In a very real sense, then, species are an invention of philosophers.

What was taken as incontrovertible was that external objects do indeed have an effect upon our outer sensory receptors, then upon our inner sense, that is, our imagination, and thereby cause sensory perception. The changes or modifications to our senses were described in terms of the senses taking species into themselves. These changes were recognised as partial causes of the kind of mental act that we call perceiving, and that our philosophers often called 'having a notion of a perceptual object'. Thus species, when in the mind, are not to be identified with notions, even though, in so far as they are present in the mind they are, like notions, qualities of a cognitive power. Species were classed by our philosophers as partial causes of notions, another partial cause being the mind itself. I shall for the present say nothing further about species, beyond noting that they resurface during the Scottish Enlightenment, when they are the subject of powerful criticism by Thomas Reid.

One further kind of partial cause should here be mentioned, namely, mental dispositions. These were discussed partly in order to make it clear that they are not notions, and partly because of their importance for the concept of memory. Mental dispositions are like notions because they are to be classed as qualities of a cognitive power. They are unlike notions because they are not themselves acts of mind, even though it is only in virtue of our mental dispositions that many of our notions exist. If I see something, or hear something, look at a tree, or have a conversation with someone, I might then put the experience to the back of my mind. It has not gone clean out of existence since it is available for recall, and therefore must in some sense be somewhere in order to be recalled. In such a state of existence it is a disposition, since it disposes the mind to act in certain ways.

Thus if I am asked what the conversation was about I am disposed to respond in a certain way since I have been prompted by my memory. But the mental disposition is not itself a mental act for the mere possession of a piece of knowledge does not imply that I am presently exercising that knowledge by thinking about it. If I do exercise the knowledge then I am having a notion, that is, engaged in a certain kind of mental act. Hence the disposition is a cause, or at least a partial cause, of the notion, without itself being a notion. For it is not active, and a notion by its nature is active.

It was routinely said that notions *represent* something or in some way to a cognitive power. To represent is to *re*-present, that is, to present again. I look at a tree and thereby have a notion of the tree. First the tree is present 'out there' and then it is present again 'in my mind'. But in what sense can the tree be present in my mind? The tree is not just a piece of matter. It also possesses something which makes that piece of matter a tree. What is it that makes a tree a *tree*? The answer standardly given was that it is a tree in virtue of having a certain form, its treeness. And while that form is not itself material it can give form to, or 'inform', what is material. Having seen the tree I can think about it, that is, have a notion of it. What makes my thought of a tree, a thought of a *tree*? The answer is that it is the very same thing that makes a tree a tree, namely, the form. That form, as already said, is not material (even though it can inform matter), and in so far as it is not material there is no difficulty in saying that it can also give form to, or inform, a mind. That is to say, the form of a tree can be in a mind no less than in matter. If I look at a tree and thereby form a notion of what I am looking at, it is one and the same form, the form of a tree, which is in the world 'out there' and also in my mind. As regards the form, therefore, the tree out there and my notion of the tree are identical. They are 'formally identical'. For this reason it makes sense to say that the notion represents the tree, and indeed, in view of the formal identity between the tree and the notion, the notion is the most appropriate representative of the tree that the tree could possibly have. For in a way the tree is thereby representing itself.

This last point sheds light on a common description given of notions. They are said to be similarities or likenesses of their objects.[39] We might well wonder how a notion of a tree can be a likeness of its object. But it is now plain that this description of notions is fitting, for the object and the notion have the same form, and things which have the same form are of course like each other. Admittedly the tree is a piece of matter, and the notion is an act of mind, and therefore not material. But, as already observed, this does not prevent the two things, one material and the other not, having the same form.

Since our philosophers regarded the notion of a perceptual object as the representative of the object, there is a sense in which they could be said to have held a 'representative theory of perception'. But the ascription to them of such a theory is misleading even though it is, strictly speaking, correct. The common account of a representative theory of perception is this: when a perceiver perceives an object the immediate object of his perceptual knowledge is not the object out there, but is instead a mental representative of that object, produced in the perceiver by the causal efficacy of the object out there. His knowledge of the object out there is through, or is mediated by, his knowledge of that mental representative. On this account there are thus two objects of perceptual knowledge, one immediate, the other mediate.

John Locke is commonly thought to have held just such a theory of perception. Locke says that 'idea' is 'that term which, I think, serves best to stand for whatsoever is the object of the understanding when a man thinks'; he uses it to signify 'whatever it is which the mind can be employed about in thinking'[40]; and he tells us that the mind perceives nothing but its own ideas. According to the view with which Locke is thus credited, we know external objects by inspecting our ideas and assuming that their cause must in some way resemble their effect. If this is how the ideas are, then this likewise is how the objects are also.

The foregoing is a very crude account of the common interpretation of Locke, and that interpretation of Locke may in any case be a travesty (as I think it is). The point to which I wish to draw attention here however is that that theory of perception, which is properly called a representative theory of perception in view of the fact that the ideas are to be thought of as representatives of their objects, is in a crucial respect utterly unlike the representative theory of perception which was held by our Pre-Reformation philosophers. For notions, which do indeed represent their objects, are not to be thought of as objects of knowledge through which we come to a perceptual grasp of the external object. On the contrary they are the perceptual acts themselves by which we reach out perceptually to the external things. In this sense notions are not intermediaries; but Lockean ideas (as interpreted above) are just such intermediaries. Notions are active, whereas Lockean ideas are passive and are themselves the objects of mental acts. These metaphysical differences between notions and Lockean ideas are so great that if it is appropriate to speak of Locke's theory of perception as a representative theory it is preferable if we do not classify the perception theory of our philosophers in the same way; two such disparate theories should not be treated as though they are basically the same. In so far as activity and passivity are opposites then so are the two kinds of perception theory just considered. In ways that matter the medieval theory we have been considering seems greatly superior to the one which I have, no doubt unfairly, attributed to Locke.

I shall turn now, though briefly, to an important difference between notions. Some are intuitive and others abstractive; this distinction is important because important philosophical insights rest upon it. I shall attend here to certain of those insights.

Lokert's definitions will suffice for present purposes: 'An intuitive notion is a notion through which a contingent truth about the notion's object can be known, for example, that it is white or seated, that it is distant or nearby, or that the object exists or does not exist. The opposite is said about an abstractive notion, viz. that through it no contingent truth can be known about its object.'[41] Some examples should make it clear what is at issue here. In looking at a tree I have a notion (a visual notion) of the tree. This notion, which we must remember is really a mental act, is my being aware of the tree. There are different ways of being aware of the tree. In virtue of the fact that I am now looking at the tree, the way I am now aware of it can be characterised by listing the truths I know about the tree as a result of my present relation to it. These truths include the following; (1) the tree exists, (2) it has green leaves, (3) its base is covered by moss. All these truths are contingent in the philosophical sense that there is no necessity that they be true and no necessity that they be false. The tree happens to exist, but it is not necessary that it exist. The tree happens to be leafy, but there is no necessity that it have leaves, and so on. A notion which yields such knowledge as that just described is said to be intuitive.

Having looked at the tree I then shut my eyes, or in some other way remove myself from sensory contact with the tree, and while thus sensorily out of contact with the tree I think about it. In thinking about it I do, of course, form a notion of it, for to think at all is to have a notion of what is being thought about. The notion I now have of the tree while out of sensory contact with it, is however of a quite different kind from the notion I had of it while looking at it. The difference can best be expressed by saying that my thinking now yields none of the contingent truths that the earlier, intuitive notion had yielded. For now, not in sensory contact with the tree, I am unable to say for certain whether the tree exists at present or not. It could have been destroyed sometime during the period, however brief, that I was not looking at it. And if it does not even exist, then the other truths earlier listed are true no longer. If a tree does not exist then it *is* not anything, and hence is not leafy either, and neither can it have a mossy base – what does not exist does not have any sort of base, though no doubt it would have one if it existed.

Thus argued our philosophers. I can of course say what I remember about the tree, and no doubt many of those things that I remember were indeed both true and contingent. But though they were true they may be true no longer. Knowledge of the kind just described involves possession of an abstractive, and not an intuitive, notion. It is called 'abstractive' because it abstracts from existence. That is to say, simply put, the notion yields no knowledge of the present existence of its object. All memory notions are of that kind.

This is plainly a technical sense of 'abstractive' and has little (though not nothing) to do with the concept of 'abstraction' which we ordinarily employ when we say that democracy, or justice, is an abstraction. The connection is, roughly, as follows: If I look at two trees, say an oak and an elm, I form an intuitive notion of those trees. I might subsequently think about each of those two trees, and I thereby form abstractive notions of them. A consideration of those two notions may cause me to have a further notion of what those two trees have in common, what was called their 'common nature', their treeness. This new abstractive notion is crucially unlike the previous two abstractive notions of the trees, for the new one is equally true of both trees, whereas the earlier notions are not; the abstractive notion of the oak is true only of the oak which gave rise to the notion of it, and the abstractive notion of the elm is true only of the elm which gave rise to the notion of it. The notion of a tree-as-such which is derived by abstraction from other notions, is a 'universal', and its status is that of what may be termed a 'second level abstractive notion'. This latter kind of abstractive notion is a good deal closer to what we have in mind when we say of something that it is only an abstraction. When we speak of democracy as an abstraction, we do not mean the democracy of Britain, or of Spain, or of the United States. We mean what it is that these three (and other) countries have in common in virtue of which we call each of them a democracy.

There is an interesting question, widely discussed, as to whether an abstractive notion of a given object must be preceded by an intuitive notion of the same object. In this context much was made of the role of imagination in the formation of our notions. Seemingly we can have a notion of a hippogryph, but not an intuitive notion of one since no such animal exists. It is then, presumably, an abstractive notion. Interesting questions arise in this context, which bear a close resemblance to questions later raised by Hume and others concerning whether to every idea there corresponds a preceding impression. I shall not follow the Pre-Reformation Scots down that road now. Instead I wish to raise a question about the relation between intuitive and abstractive notions in respect of their proper objects.

Suppose I look at a tree, and then think about the tree though I am no longer in sensory contact with it. I thus have first an intuitive, and then an abstractive notion of it. What is the immediate object of those two notions? Is it the same object in the two cases? On this matter more than one view was canvassed. Some held that the immediate object of the abstractive notion is different, on the grounds that whereas in an obvious way the immediate object of the intuitive notion is the tree itself, the immediate object of the abstractive notion is the species in the mind which is the mental representative of the tree and through which we have a notion of the tree. According to this view the notion of the tree is mediated by a notion of the species. One conclusion drawn from this is that every abstractive notion of an external object is also intuitive since the abstractive notion of the object involves intuitive knowledge of the species of the object. It is intuitive knowledge of the species since it gives rise to knowledge of contingent truths, in particular the contingent truth that the species exists.

John Mair did not like this story at all. Why, after all, invoke the species in this context? Perhaps it is in order to ensure that the mind is in immediate cognitive contact with the representative of the absent object. But how can we judge that the species does represent what it is supposed to unless we are also in direct cognitive contact with the object itself? And if we are in such contact with the object then there is no point in invoking the species. The job that the species was invoked to do is a job that does not require to be done. If I am thinking about Glasgow Cathedral then the cathedral is immediately present to my thought though not to my senses. There is perhaps in my mind a species of the building, but if so then the species is that by which I am thinking of the building. I am not after all thinking about the species, for I am thinking about a seven centuries old building and my species is not that. It is with considerations such as these in mind that Mair asserts: 'In vain is it laid down that through the same notion we know two objects, one intuitively and the other abstractively, since everything could be maintained by saying that through that notion by itself the external object is known.'[42] What Mair says on this matter seems common sense. And the particular common-sensical point that he makes here links him directly, as we shall see, with the Scottish common sense school which flourished two and a half centuries later.

Much was made of the distinction between grasping something and judging, or passing judgement on, it. If I see or hear the term 'tree' I shall perhaps form a notion of a tree. Having that notion does not in itself imply that I am judging anything. But if I am looking at a tree and a person points to it and says 'That tree is leafy' I not only have a notion of what he said, in that I grasped the signification of it; I also judge what he says, for if I can see leaves on the tree I will assent to the proposition just uttered, and if I see no leaves on the tree I will dissent. Grasping the signification of a proposition and judging the proposition are two distinct acts, for I can grasp a proposition while having no idea whether the proposition is true or false, and that is to say that I do not judge it. Two kinds of act of judgement were generally recognised, assent and dissent, that is, saying 'yes' and saying 'no'. And these two kinds of act were classed as two kinds of notion, two kinds of 'judicative' notion. Since grasping the signification of a proposition is also having a notion, an 'apprehensive propositional notion', it follows that when I give my assent to a proposition there are in fact two notions in my mind, the first is the apprehensive notion and the second the judicative. I say 'first' because there is a natural order of priority in this. In some sense of 'first' I must grasp the proposition first, for otherwise there is nothing for me to assent to.

It is necessary however to refine this last point, for there was discussion about articles of faith concerning the mysteries of the Church, where the faithful as an act of faith said 'yes' without grasping the signification of the propositions. But, of course, the matter is not so clear cut, for there are degrees of apprehension, and that the faithful do not have a full apprehension of certain of the articles of faith does not imply that they have no idea at all what it is to which they are giving their assent. We shall return to this point later. Here I wish only to note that since in giving assent to a proposition the mind must be directed to that pro-position in so far as it is understood, it follows that the relation between an assent and its attendant apprehensive notion is the relation between an act and its object. Just as anger requires an object, and as love requires one, so also assent requires one, and its object is a notion. There is nothing paradoxical about a notion having another notion as its object.

There is however one conspicuous difficulty in this area which should be acknowledged. Let us accept, as members of Mair's circle accepted, that an apprehensive notion of a proposition, and a judicative notion by which I assent to that proposition, are in reality distinct notions. There is a fundamental thesis of medieval theology that if two things are really distinct then it is possible for God to destroy one while preserving the other. For example, let us suppose that ordinarily if a given stone is placed close by a fire the stone will get hot. Since the temperature of the stone is really distinct from the heat of the fire, it is possible for God to prevent the stone getting hot even though the adjacent fire continues to burn. The parallel situation in which we are interested is this: since an assent is a notion which is really distinct from the proposition to which the assent is given, or, put otherwise, is really distinct from the apprehensive notion by which I grasp the sense of a proposition, then it is possible for God to preserve the assent while destroying the apprehension of the proposition to which assent is given.[43] The outcome of such a divine act is that I give assent without there being anything to which I assent. There is no doubt that this is hard doctrine, though George Lokert subscribed to it. I have argued elsewhere that the doctrine is philosophically untenable though it is not absolutely to be ruled out if considered within a theological context.[44] I shall not pursue that deep matter here, but shall instead take up an important matter relating to a principle of division, not yet considered, between varieties of assent. The distinction now at issue is that between evident assent and inevident assent. Consideration of this matter will take us into strange areas.

5 Ways of Saying 'Yes'

In this chapter we shall attend to the distinction between evident and inevident assent. There was not total agreement about how 'evident' and 'inevident' should be defined, but Mair's exposition is to be found in many other writers also. He tells us that evident assent is assent which is true, unhesitant, caused by principles which necessitate the intellect, and in thus assenting the intellect cannot be deceived.[45] Highest evident assent is evident assent of such a nature that the assenter, in thus assenting, cannot be deceived even by God. Natural evident assent is evident assent of such a nature that though the assenter can be deceived as a result of a special act of God, he cannot be deceived by natural means, or by what was termed 'the general and routine influence of God'.[46] An example commonly given of highest evident assent is the assenter's assent to the proposition 'I exist'. The proposition is contingent, that is, it is neither necessary nor impossible that it be true, for it affirms the existence of a being whose existence is neither necessary nor impossible. Necessary propositions, that is, propositions which are true and cannot be false, also, and not surprisingly, are proper objects of highest evident assent. Lokert asserts that there is no necessary proposition which is given anything but highest evident assent.[47]

There are important things going on in the dictum of Lokert's just referred to. Earlier a distinction was drawn between three kinds of language, spoken, written, and mental. Propositions can be considered likewise under one or other of those three heads of division. When Lokert states that no necessary proposition can be given anything but highest evident assent, he cannot have had either spoken or written necessary propositions in mind.

For a person might misunderstand a necessary proposition and withhold evident assent to it; he might indeed think the proposition is false. Lokert must therefore have been thinking of mental propositions only. The stock example of a necessary proposition was 'Every whole is greater than any part of it'. If I grasp this proposition correctly then the mental proposition which I have is no less a necessary proposition than the written one I have correctly grasped. But if I have misunderstood the written proposition then the mental proposition, which is my mental act of grasping the written one, may not be a necessary one and therefore there is no difficulty in seeing why I might have withheld evident assent from the proposition, or even dissented from it. But my correct grasp of a necessary written proposition, say 'Every whole is greater than any of its parts', is another matter. According to Lokert my assent to it is caused by causes which necessitate my intellect. The causes are so powerful that it is impossible for them to be overridden by anything else. What Lokert is saying is that not even God can prevent me from giving assent to a necessary mental proposition.

This is a tough doctrine. It sets a clear limit on the power of God to prevent a human act. And it was no doubt in the light of this theological aspect to the doctrine that some philosophers objected, as Lokert was well aware, to his position on this matter. They invoked a theological principle we have already found it necessary to attend to, namely, that of two things which are really distinct from each other it is possible for God to destroy either while preserving the other. The two things here are two notions, first the apprehensive propositional notion, which is my act of correctly grasping the sense of a necessary proposition, and secondly the judicative notion which is my act of assenting to that first notion. An immediate implication of the theological principle just stated is that God can preserve in existence my correct grasp of the sense of a necessary proposition while destroying my assent to that proposition. In that case it would have to be concluded that there could be no such thing as highest evident assent.

The doctrine of highest evident assent has a heroic aspect at which we can only marvel. Necessary propositions, or at least necessary mental propositions, should not be considered merely passive things upon which we act in some way. As mental propositions they are essentially active, they are the mind acting, apprehending, making sense of something. They are also active in that they have causal efficacy. They can so act upon the mind as to produce assent. And in a sense the power of a necessary mental proposition has to be considered to be infinite. For so great is that power to produce assent that not even God can do anything to prevent it securing its effect. This is truly an awesome feature of necessary propositions.

I do not wish to say that God could not prevent us assenting to a necessary proposition. He could prevent us by the simple expedient of preventing us from attending to it, though it has to be said that we do not need to invoke the power of God to explain how we might be diverted from giving assent to a necessary proposition; we could divert ourselves, by will or inadvertently. The important point here is that God cannot prevent our giving assent to a necessary proposition during the time that we are attending to that proposition and correctly grasping its sense.

But if we say that the power of a necessary mental proposition is infinite in the way described, we have to note that in a sense the opposite should be said about the very cognitive power whose act is that necessary proposition. For if the power of the proposition is infinite, then our power to resist that proposition is itself infinitesimal. Or perhaps it should be said that in the face of a necessary proposition we are simply powerless. Nothing would count as trying to avoid giving assent, for the necessary proposition would totally overwhelm the will. And in a sense that is what we should expect. For if the infinite power of God's will is insufficient to prevent a necessary proposition securing our assent, then we have no right to suppose that our own will would do any better.

The contrast with our own will in another of its operations could hardly be stronger, for our will is itself in a sense infinite. Whenever we do something by an act of will, say pick up a pencil, what thereby happens is not what would have happened if we had not acted by will but instead nature had been allowed to take its course. Thus it can be said that whenever we do anything by will, we set ourselves against the whole of nature. And win. It is not at all inappropriate to conclude that in this respect our will, though a merely human power, is nevertheless infinite – not infinite in the way that God's is, but infinite all the same. Yet our will, which manifests such power when dealing with the system of nature, is utterly powerless when faced with a necessary proposition, even such a simple little thing as that two plus two equals four. How can we understand that proposition and not say yes to it!

There is a point closely related to the considerations just presented, which I want to raise now partly because of its intrinsic interest, and partly because it directly concerns a matter which surfaced during the Enlightenment and then assumed the greatest significance. We saw that there are two kinds of evident assent, evident assent where I cannot be deceived so long as nature runs its routine course, and evident assent where I cannot be deceived even if God seeks to interfere with nature's routine. As regards the former kind of case, I might give evident assent and yet be deceived because God is causing me to be deceived. We must grant therefore that I might by God's will give evident assent to something and in so doing be deceived. But a theologian would know that we could not in any given case rule out the possibility that God had taken a hand in the course of nature precisely in order to change that course (as would happen if he destroyed a substance and preserved its qualities). In that case why give evident assent to any proposition except necessary ones? We have already seen that we cannot help giving assent to necessary propositions, but what about all those evident assents which arise as a product of our intuitive notions of objects in the external world? In such cases there is surely room for the will to be exercised to prevent our evident assent, and in the light of the theologian's knowledge of the possibility that we might actually be being deceived when we look out upon the world and pass judgement about what there is out there, why is the will not in fact exercised to prevent our evident assent?

I think that there is an obvious answer to this problem. It is that we give evident assent to propositions about the existence and properties of things in the external world because it is our nature to do so. Of course I know that I may be in error in thinking that I am holding a pencil. But my awareness of this theoretical possibility (theoretical, because it is accepted as an implication of a theory) carries no implication for my practical living. Though knowing certain philosophical and theological positions, I do not in fact believe that I am being deceived when I think I am holding a pencil. The proof of this is my behaviour. If I thought that I were possibly not holding a pencil I might seek to do something about it, for instance, go off in search of another pencil, or try using the one I think I am holding to see if it really exists. But of course I am not going to do any such thing. I know the pencil is there because I am looking at it. The will plays no role in my assent. My nature forces my assent upon me, whatever theologians might say.

I have spoken at some length about the power of mental propositions to produce assent in us, and I said that we are entitled to regard necessary propositions as bearers of infinite power in the light of their ability to secure their effect even against God's will (should He ever will to block their exercise of power). But we should not lose sight of a metaphysical point concerning the mode of existence of necessary mental propositions. They have, as already said, the status of mental acts. They do not last forever. While the person is thinking about the necessary proposition, that proposition exists. When he ceases to think about it, it is no longer in his mind, or anywhere else either. His ceasing to think about it is a way of destroying it. It does not take much to destroy a necessary mental proposition; the person has merely to think about something else, and it is gone. Thus the mode of existence of the proposition is not such as to justify describing it as necessary; its existence is a purely contingent matter. It happens to exist and just as easily might happen not to exist, and when it exists it does not do so by its own efforts. A proposition has absolutely no resources within itself to heave itself into existence, and it has none to prevent the thinker from diverting his attention to some other matter and thereby annihilating that proposition. There is a strange and awesome contrast concerning necessary mental propositions. They have the power to secure the assent of the thinker, even against God's will and yet they have no power on their own account to exist at all, never mind to exist necessarily. Metaphysically, a necessary proposition, despite its causal power, is all but nothing.

I have so far had a good deal to say about evident assent, but of course not all assent is evident. Two kinds of inevident assent were discussed rather fully. One is opinion, and the other is the assent of faith. The reason opinion (or an 'opinative notion' as it was sometimes called) is classed as inevident assent is that to opine is to give hesitant assent, whereas evident assent is firm. It might be replied that some opinions are held with the utmost conviction, but it should be noted that among our philosophers 'opinion' was routinely used as a technical term, which was taken to signify a proposition which is, among other things, naturally caused and hesitant.

The second kind of inevident assent I mentioned above is the assent of faith. Assent of faith was taken to be assent to a truth. Beyond that it was said to be firm and to be freely caused, that is, caused by an act of will. In so far as it is firm it is unlike opinion, and in so far as it is freely caused it is unlike either evident assent or opinion. It was held almost universally that there is a conceptual link between faith and will. There is indeed ample scriptural warrant for linking the two and that warrant was duly discussed. Most notably, the verse 'He who does not believe will be condemned' [Mark 16:16] was quoted in support of the position. Mair, for example, argues that it is therefore a precept that we believe, but nothing is a precept unless the will cooperate in its implementation.[48] He speaks about faith as a perfection of the will.[49] What he appears to mean by this is that the will's power is actualised or perfected in its exercise, and an assent of faith requires just such an exercise.

Of course, it might be argued that in important respects an assent of faith is anything but perfect, for there is only imperfect evidence for the proposition to which an assent of faith is given. If there were conclusive evidence, that is to say, if the truth of the proposition could be demonstrated then there would be no need for the will to be exercised in order for the assent to be forthcoming. Faced with a demonstration of the truth of the proposition the mind would respond in the way that it responds to any necessary proposition, namely, by giving assent by nature. In that case it is not merely that the will would not be needed to secure assent; there would in fact be no room for the will to play any role whatever. As soon as the demonstration is grasped, the assent is forthcoming. It might therefore be said that the need for an act of will to produce assent shows up the imperfection in the assent.

But it might be said that we should draw the opposite conclusion. For it is the easiest thing in the world to give assent to a necessary proposition. As already observed, there is nothing whatever that we have to do in order to give that assent beyond actually grasping the sense of the proposition. We grasp its sense and so to say sit back and let nature take its course. What could be easier than doing nothing? Assenting to a necessary proposition is nothing to boast about if nobody who grasps the proposition could fail to assent. But an assent of faith is an entirely different matter. In such a case it is never just a matter of grasping a proposition, settling back, and letting nature takes its course. The human spirit has in addition to exert itself in an act of will. Thus for an assent of faith more of the human person is brought into play than is the case with evident assent, and in that sense we might say that an assent of faith is the more perfect of the two kinds of assent. It represents, in a way, a triumph of the spirit – though it should be stressed that while evident assent does not require an act of will once the sense of the proposition is grasped, it may take an almost superhuman effort of will to get oneself into a position to grasp the sense of the proposition, and in that case we are no less entitled to regard such assent also as a triumph of the human spirit. And indeed, to take the opposite kind of case, rather than fight his way to the kind of grasp of a proposition that produces an evident assent a person might abandon that goal and settle, too readily, for assenting to the proposition as an act of faith. He has taken the easy way out and his assent is certainly less to be regarded as a triumph of the spirit than is the assent of a person who has striven, in the end successfully, for a full grasp of the proposition's sense.

A point, previously hinted at, should here be made explicit. That is that while we do not have an irresistible reason for accepting the truth of a proposition to which an assent of faith is given, we do have some reason for accepting it, though not an irresistible one.[50] All our philosophers held that if there is no reason whatever to accept a proposition then our acceptance of it should not count as an assent of faith. There has thus to be what they termed a 'probable' reason for assenting to it, that is, a reason on the basis of which we can say that there is some degree of probability that the proposition is actually true. Hence to give an assent of faith to a proposition is not a wholly irrational act. There is some reason, that is, rational justification, for it. On the basis of this consideration some of our philosophers said that we cannot give an assent of faith to a proposition unless we would accept the proposition as one of our opinions (in the technical sense, mentioned earlier, of that term).

One important kind of justification is the word of an authority.[51] Examples not taken from religious faith will do as well as any. If someone sees an event and subsequently tells me what he saw, I may well believe that the event did happen. But my assent is not like the assent that I would have given to the proposition if I had seen the event myself. In the latter case my assent would have been evident assent, for I would have been wholly unable not to say yes to the proposition. In the case where someone gives me an eyewitness account, on the other hand, my acceptance is in part an act of faith, for I have to trust the person. There are clearly different degrees of justification for trusting someone. A person whom I have known for a long time, and who to the best of my considerable knowledge has never spoken falsely to me, better merits my trust than does someone I hardly know at all, or simply don't know at all. Religious authorities are likewise placed in relation to my assent. I might accept someone's word because he was an eyewitness, or because he himself had accepted the word of an eyewitness, and so on. And if there were many who claim to have witnessed an event this no doubt will in most cases increase the likelihood that the event did take place, and therefore strengthen the rational basis of my assent to the proposition that it took place.

This way of putting the matter prompts the question of how strong the rational basis of the assent should be before I am entitled to exercise my will and give an assent of faith. I should like to close this chapter with a brief word on this matter.[52] A central feature of Aristotle's ethical theory is his doctrine of the mean, according to which any virtue occurs on an intermediate point of a spectrum at whose extremes is a vice. Thus in relation to any virtue there are two vices which in one sense are opposite to each other and which, in another sense, are both opposite to the virtue. Thus for example the virtue of courage is said to be a mean between cowardice and rashness, and liberality to be a mean between extravagance and meanness. Of any pair of vices in relation to a given mean, one of the vices is an excess and the other a deficiency. For example, in an obvious sense, rashness is an excess in relation to courage, and cowardice a deficiency. Of course, it is necessary to specify the quality or qualities in respect of which a vice is an excess or a deficiency. I do not wish here to enter the lists on behalf of one or another of the many competing interpretations and defences of this doctrine, but shall merely say that even if Aristotle's doctrine is not universally true, it is true for many virtues, and it is often helpful, for philosophical purposes, to consider a virtue in its relation to vices which do indeed seem to stand, as Aristotle says, as extremes in relation to the virtuous mean.

A feature of all virtues, in Aristotle's view, is that they are dispositions of the soul of a rational person. Exercise of virtue is always and necessarily an exercise of reason, whether practical reason, as in the case of the moral virtues (such as courage and justice), or theoretical reason, as in the case of the intellectual virtues (such as scientific knowledge and philosophical wisdom). Within this schema for virtues and vices it is possible to place the virtue of reasonable faith.

To see this, let us begin by reminding ourselves that our philosophers held that unless there is some evidence for a given proposition we cannot have faith in it. For those philosophers, blind faith, that is, faith in a proposition which one had absolutely no reason to accept, is not possible. They did not deny that assent can be given to a proposition purely by an act of will and without the benefit of any evidence. But they preferred not to call such an assent an assent of faith. But even if there is some evidence for a proposition it might still be so meagre as to entail that anyone who gives an assent of faith on the basis of that evidence is credulous. His faith is unreasonable because he has insufficient rational ground for giving his assent. On the other hand a person might be faced with very strong evidence for a given proposition, evidence which makes it very highly probable indeed that the proposition is true. If he nevertheless refuses to give an assent of faith to the proposition we should say that he is being unreasonable in his unbelief. That is, he suffers from incredulity – a refusal to believe when it is reasonable, in the light of the evidence, to give assent. This would be the case if, say, a person refused to accept anyone's eyewitness report, however good the track record of the witness; the incredulous person would insist that he would require to be a witness himself to give assent. In the case of a theological or religious proposition he might even insist that if he cannot be an eyewitness then a demonstration is the only thing which would satisfy him.

Thus we find that the virtue of reasonable faith can be placed between the vice of credulity (which is unreasonable believing) and the vice of incredulity (which is unreasonable non-believing). Credulity is the extreme of excess and incredulity the extreme of deficiency. Where on this scale we should place reasonable faith cannot be stated in any precise terms. The situation is no different for reasonable faith than for the other virtues. Aristotle stated that the position of a virtue in relation to two flanking vices could not be calculated as if one were faced with a problem in arithmetic. One consideration here was that a given virtue might lie closer to one of the extremes than to the other, as for example courage lying, as Aristotle thought, closer to rashness than to cowardice, and liberality lying closer to extravagance than to meanness. But how much closer depended greatly upon the particular psychological make-up of the individual. One person might find it harder to overcome a tendency to cowardice than might another, and in that sense the cowardice of the first lies further from the virtue of courage than is the case as regards the second person. Given that there are so many variables and imponderables, it is necessary for the person to have *aisthesis*, that is, a faculty of judgement by which, having lived long enough and having reflected intelligently upon the human condition in its manifold aspects, a person comes to have a sense of what is relevant and of what matters most in deciding what, in a given circumstance, he should do to remain faithful to his rational nature.

The same thing has to be said about reasonable faith in relation to credulousness and incredulousness. To put the matter in modern terms, there is no algorithm enabling us to be virtuous. Virtue has to be worked for by the exertion of will, not only as regards bringing ourselves to do what we know we ought, but also as regards our discovering what it is that we ought to do in order to remain faithful to our rational nature. Our philosophers, who wrote extensively on ethical matters, never lost sight of this aspect of the burden of our freedom. In the next chapter we shall turn to a brief discussion of part of their account of human freedom. As we shall see, questions relating to human knowledge are an important part of that account.

6 Free Will and Grace

Problems relating to free will and grace play as important a part in the writings of Mair's friend and colleague William Manderston as they do in the writings of John Ireland. In this chapter I shall deal with certain aspects of Manderston's discussions in this area. His doctrines in this field must take on an added significance for those interested in the history of Scottish culture in view of the fact that one of his students at the University of Paris was Patrick Hamilton (1503–1528), theologian and reformer, and proto-martyr of the Scottish Reformation. I shall mention very briefly some of the relevant historical background here, for the fact that Hamilton had this relation with Manderston in particular and also, more generally, with Mair's circle in St Andrews as well as in Paris, suggests important lines of research into the intellectual origins of the Scottish Reformation.

Hamilton received his MA in Paris in 1520. He then attended the University of Louvain, and in 1523 matriculated at the University of St Andrews. Three years later he began to proclaim the new faith and in 1527 fled to the Continent with Gilbert Winram, a Lothian man who had a similar reason for fearing for his well-being in Scotland. The two men briefly attended the new university at Marburg,[53] where Hamilton wrote a thesis under the ex-Franciscan François Lambert. The thesis was written in Latin, but the English reformer John Frith translated part of it into English, and the translation was published in 1529. The translation came to acquire the title *Patrick's Places*, though it is possible that Hamilton was not responsible for the title. Nor can it be wholly ruled out that Frith took liberties with the text while making the translation. Certainly some of the passages would appear strange in a modern doctoral thesis, especially the passages of litany such as:

> The Law showeth us,
> Our sin.
> Our condemnation:
> Is the word of ire.
> Is the word of despair.
> Is the word of displeasure.
> The Gospel showeth us,
> A remedy for it.
> Our redemption:
> Is the word of grace.
> Is the word of comfort.
> Is the word of peace.

Nevertheless Hamilton's passionate commitment to his new faith might have led him to use just such language, even in his thesis, if he thought that by such means some other person might thereby be brought to see the light which also guided Hamilton. Whatever the truth of the matter, Frith's translation of that part of the thesis was in due course incorporated by Knox into his *History of the Reformation in Scotland*.[54] It was in that context that Hamilton as a theologian came to have his chief influence. Here I shall restrict myself to a consideration of the relation between Hamilton's ideas on free will and grace and Manderston's ideas in that same field.[55]

The concept of appetite [*appetitus*] retained for medieval philosophers, as it retains for us, a link with its etymological root, which is the concept of seeking something out. We are familiar with appetite, and use the term in a rather wide way so that it covers not just the human body's natural tendency to seek out food but also our natural tendency to seek out many other kinds of things in response to a felt need. Manderston, in keeping with the Aristotelian tradition which he inherited, was more generous than we are in his view of the kinds of things that can be said to have appetites. We would say that animals (ourselves included) have appetite, but that plants do not. Manderston would disagree. He speaks in the *Bipartitum* of 'natural appetite', which is the natural inclination that something has to its own perfection. All natural things have such an appetite. Even dead matter can be thought of as having it in so far as it has a nature in relation to which it has a proper end. Thus water and earth have a natural inclination to descend in virtue of their gravity or weight, and fire and air have a natural inclination to rise because that is their nature. Their proper place is above. This view, inherited from Aristotelian physics, may seem unimpressive now. There is more plausibility in talking about natural appetite in the case of all sorts of living things, for example, plants seeking the sun, and drawing up nutrients from the soil.

It is plain that such appetite does not presuppose cognition but the other two kinds of appetite discussed do require it. The sensitive appetite is the faculty which an animal possesses by nature by which the animal pursues what is agreeable to it, and flees from what is disagreeable. Manderston speaks of five outer sense appetites, one corresponding to each sensory receptor, and an inner sense appetite, which corresponds to the imagination (which is called, however misleadingly, an inner sense.) I do not think there is merit in probing the details of this aspect of his theory, and shall focus instead upon the third of the three kinds of appetite he discusses, namely, rational appetite, also called 'will'. Just as the sensitive appetite moves the agent by nature, so the will moves the agent freely. By an act of will the agent freely pursues or flees its object.

Manderston's concept of will lies at the heart of his moral philosophy. The main moral philosophical concept that he explores is 'virtue', and wishing to determine where virtue stands in the scheme of things he asks in which faculty of the soul virtue, considered subjectively, should be placed.[56] His reply is that it should be placed in the will. Virtue is classed as a certain kind of disposition of the soul, for it disposes us to will actions. Virtue, then, is a disposition of the will. It is for this reason that Manderston says that will is the place of virtue.

Both sensitive appetite and rational appetite presuppose cognition; a beast does not pursue its prey if it does not know it is there. Even less do we will if we do not know what our will is directed to – nothing is willed unless already known [*nihil volitum nisi praecognitum*]. Manderston, with liberal use of metaphor, tells us that will is blind in its operations and its adviser is intellect, for the will pursues or flees no object unless the intellect shows that the object is something to be pursued or avoided. Such an object can stand in one or other of two relations to the will, and on that basis two kinds of act of will are to be distinguished. They are intention and choice.[57] To intend is to will an end, by which act the will reaches out to the object for the sake of the attainment of the object. To choose is to will an end, by which act the will reaches out to the object for the sake of something other than the object. For example, if by an act of will a person loves God above all else, then that act of love is his intention. But if, out of this love, he wills to aid a pauper or to say Matins, then those acts of will are choices; for they are done not for their own sake but out of love of God.

Whether we speak about intention or choice, that is, whether what is willed is willed for its own sake or for the sake of something else, the end which is willed must be classed as a final cause. It is a cause in the sense of 'that for the sake of which' something is done. Now, final causes are most obviously to be contrasted with 'efficient causes'. An efficient cause is that from which comes the immediate origin of a movement or cessation. Thus the player who kicks the football is the efficient cause of the motion of the ball, and the person who gives advice is the efficient cause of the act which duly embodies that advice. The act of the efficient cause which produces the efficient effect, is antecedent to that effect. In contrast, the final cause is to be conceived of as the end aimed at. For example, if I seek health by taking exercise, then the health at which I aim is the final cause of my exercise.

But the concept of a final cause must be seen to give rise to a problem for if I, who am not healthy, exercise for the sake of my health, then the health for the sake of which I exercise is in a clear sense the cause of my exertions, and yet the hoped-for health does not, when I begin my exercises, exist. It is, after all, what I am hoping will exist after I have exercised. This fact prompts a question: how can what does not exist be a cause? The desired end causes the act of will, but if the desired end does not exist, then surely it cannot cause anything, nor therefore cause an act of will either.

Manderston addresses this problem. His answer is that what does not exist cannot cause anything. When we refer to the causality of a final cause, what we have in mind is the efficient causality of an act of the appetitive power, where that power acts, not blindly, but on the advice of the intellect which has presented to the appetitive power the concept of something worthy of pursuit. Strictly, therefore, what moves the agent is not the end (which does not yet exist) but the willing of the end.

Our willing an end does not of course imply that the end will be achieved. One aspect of the infinite will of God is that there is no conceivable obstacle to the realisation of any end willed by God. Whether we secure an end willed is always a contingent matter. However, a distinction of prime importance in canon law as well as in ethics must be noted here. It is that between two kinds of act of will.

Manderston considers the act of walking. There are two aspects to the walking, the internal and the external. The internal aspect upon which Manderston wishes to focus is the act of will which is the efficient cause of the physical act. The external aspect is the effect of that efficient cause, namely, the walking.

The walking can itself fairly be described as an act, and in that case there are two acts at issue, first the act of will by which the agent wills to walk, and secondly the act which constitutes in a sense the embodiment of that act. Using terminology made famous by St Thomas Aquinas, Manderston distinguishes between the elicited act [*actus elicitus*] which is the act of will by which the agent wills to walk, and the commanded act [*actus imperatus*] which is the walking.[58] These two acts stand in different relations to the will for though the walking is willed the willing is not, since the agent did not will to will – he willed to walk. The elicited act is to be thought of as a command; the agent, in willing, commands himself to walk; and the commanded act is to be thought of as an act of obedience to that self-directed command.

This version of the 'command theory of the will' has a great deal to commend it. This is not perhaps the place to enter into a detailed examination of the theory, but I should like at least to stay for the present with the distinction between the elicited act and the commanded act, and to make a point regarding the order of priority. Manderston's claim is that of the two kinds of act, internal and external, it is the internal that is free in the primary sense, and the external, the willed act, is free in a merely derivative or secondary sense. To say that the commanded act is free is to say that it is performed in response to a command which is itself freely given. Hence the freedom of the commanded act is vicarious and is a dependent freedom. Part of the justification for this claim is that the commanded act could in fact have been performed without having been commanded by the will, that is, it could have been performed without a preceding elicited act. In such a case the exterior act would not have been free. On the other hand, an elicited act can be performed by a human agent without causing a commanded act. As noted above, the human will is fallible in respect of its causal power, but the failure of the commanded act to materialise does not mean that the elicited act was not free, even less that it did not after all occur. Since the elicited act is free even if the commanded act does not occur, but the commanded act is not free unless preceded by an elicited act, it is clearly appropriate to speak about the elicited act as free primarily, and the commanded act as free only secondarily.

One might wonder whether Ockham's razor ought not to be used against this conceptual scheme. Are there not too many acts of will here? Why accept that there is an elicited act and also a commanded act? Why not say that there is just one act, the exterior act that the agent performs; and that to speak of the exterior act as a commanded act in relation to an elicited act, is just to indicate the way in which the exterior act was performed, namely, willingly? To do something by will and to do it willingly are the same thing, it might be said, and hence, instead of vainly positing the existence of an elicited act we should seek to give an account of the particular kind of modification of an act that justifies us in using the adverb 'willingly' of it. It may not be difficult to give such an account. We can say, for example, that the principle of action must be internal to the agent; that is, that there are not external pressures compelling or constraining the action. And we should add that the agent in some sense performs the act knowingly, though what precisely he has to know if his act is to be done willingly could no doubt become a matter for dispute. These suggestions are all deeply imbedded in the philosophical tradition that Manderston inherited, and derive from Aristotle's discussion, in *Nicomachean Ethics* III, 1, of the concept of 'the voluntary'.

But there is good reason to believe that despite its merits Manderston would not go along the road just sign-posted. For he held that will is not present only in overt action. He was alive to the fact that our will to perform act A may not be followed by the performance of A, whether because of an external obstacle to the performance (for example, our failure to walk because our legs are bound together), or because of an internal obstacle, as appears to happen in cases of weakness of will. Hence it is reasonable to posit elicited acts, despite Ockhamist pressures not to multiply entities beyond necessity. I think Manderston's short reply to the Ockhamist is that the positing of elicited acts really is necessary if we are to explain familiar phenomena, such as weakness of will.

Elicited acts are commonly distinguished in terms of whether they direct the agent towards or away from the object of will. The former kind of act is called 'volition' and the latter 'nolition', these being related in much the same way that affirmation and denial are related. Indeed, volition and nolition are sometimes spoken of as affirmation and denial in the will. A metaphysical point, closely connected to one just discussed, arises here. To say that something is an object of an elicited act is to say that it is volited or is nolited. The object of an affirmation or a denial is the proposition which is affirmed or denied. One difference between these two kinds of object is that a proposition cannot be affirmed or denied unless it exists, whereas something cannot be volited or nolited unless it does not, at the time of the act of will, exist; if it already exists then it is too late to will it. The will is antecedent to its object, and the agent's purpose is to produce the object by the act of will. Nevertheless what is willed must be present to the mind if it is to be willed, for, as already stated, nothing is willed unless it is already known – there is no such thing as blind willing. On this basis we can accept that there is a deeper similarity between affirming and willing, for the proposition must be present to the mind if it is to be affirmed exactly as the willed object must be.

It appears to be Manderston's view that the question of the extent of the dominion of the will is an empirical one, in the sense that we have to rely on experience to determine the answer; non-empirical means, such as conceptual analysis, cannot settle the question. In support of this account of Manderston's view it can be pointed out that he is at some pains to answer the question whether the will has dominion over the vegetative faculty (the faculty governing nutrition, growth, and digestion), over the outer sensory power (sight, hearing, and so on), over the imagination, over the intellect, and over the power of loco-motion. Yet in none of these cases does he offer a conceptual or logical justification for his answer. His view evidently is that that is just how things are. For example, we just find it to be the case that the will has no dominion over the vegetative power, but does to a certain extent (which we shall duly consider) over the intellect.

What he has to say about the will's dominion over our power of locomotion is of great interest, as linking late medieval theories of will with contemporary concerns in physics. The link is the concept of impetus. Aristotle had difficulty in accounting for the fact that a projectile continues in motion after it has left the projector, for Aristotle was committed to the view that violent motion, which is motion contrary to the nature of the thing moved, requires contact between mover and moved. Aristotle attempted to deal with the problem by saying that the mover passed on to the medium through which the moved object was passing a motive power which enabled the medium to act as the contiguous mover. Thus the hand which throws the stone into the air passes a motive power into the air surrounding the stone, and the air thereupon takes over the role which the hand had performed in getting the stone moving.

This theory found favour with few, and was replaced by the theory that the projector impressed upon the projectile a motive power that in turn maintained the projectile in flight. This impressed motive power was termed 'impetus' by John Buridan (*c.*1295 – after 1358), and subsequent discussion of impetus owed a great deal to his speculations.[59] His view of the motion of the heavenly bodies involved an account of inertia; he held that God impressed the quality of impetus upon the heavenly bodies and that that quality will not be expended. Thus it was Buridan's view that, at least as regards certain bodies, their natural state is a state of motion rather than of rest. From the scientific point of view what would require explanation would be the fact that the object stopped.

Perhaps it is merely a matter of emphasis, but later writers, with members of Mair's circle to the fore, tended to focus attention upon problems of terrestial rather than celestial mechanics, and discussed the fact that impetus is expended in projectiles. Should we say, for example, that the reason the projectile falls back to the ground is that its impetus has been destroyed by the projectile's weight? The notion of a self-expending impetus is relevant to Manderston's account of the will. That he is thinking in terms of impetus is signalled when he affirms: 'How the will, by means of its acts, causes the motions of limbs is a small problem in natural philosophy, for we often see a motion continue when the will has ceased'. This is clearly a problem conceived along the lines of the classical problem of how a projectile manages to keep moving when the projector is no longer moving it. The application to will is explicit in Manderston: 'I say that the will, by means of its act commanding that the motion be made, impresses upon the whole body a certain impetus which moves the whole body; and with this impetus remaining and the volition ceasing, the impetus will move the whole body.'[60] This is not to imply that Manderston has a physicalist account of the mind, but he must have been aware that there is something less amazing in the idea that a physical body can impress impetus upon a physical body than in the idea that an immaterial faculty of the soul can do the same thing. His remark that the impetus is impressed in an orderly way, first upon the heart and spirits, then upon the cerebrum, then the neck, and so on, does not address the question of how the will can impress a physical quality upon something if the will is not itself physical.

It should perhaps be added as clarification that Manderston is not thinking merely of cases where the body, set in motion by an act of will, is committed to completing the motion, with the will having no role to play once the motion begins, as when by an act of will we start to take a step forward and the whole weight of the body commits us to completing the motion and the will can do nothing to prevent it, or when by will we leap into the air and the body must then complete the motion that it has started though the will is no longer able to play a role. Manderston is thinking of the elicited act, which in his view takes place before the overt motion; the elicited act impresses the quality of impetus upon the body so that the body is set in motion. Thus, on this picture the elicited act finishes before the commanded act starts, and the motion of the commanded act is to be explained in terms of the impetus in the body.

We are once again dealing with the problem of action at a distance, though the distance is now temporal rather than spatial. The elicited act occurs, and sometime later the act commanded by the elicited act is still in progress. How is it possible for the effect of the elicited act to be in progress while its cause is no longer in existence? I suppose that the answer which Manderston gives could be expressed, using characteristic terminology of the late medieval philosophers, by saying that though the elicited act no longer exists, its representative, namely, the impetus imparted to the body, does exist and ensures that the body continues to move.

For example, I might will to go for a walk, and then walk. The elicited act is over before the walking, the commanded act, starts. The impetus to go for a walk is imparted to, or impressed upon, the body and then I walk. But this is not to say that the commanded act is out of my control once the walking starts and is instead in the control of the impetus. That is altogether too simplistic a picture. For my will does not go to sleep when the walking starts. I continue to reflect upon my acts and if I do not like what is happening I can will to stop them. To stay within Manderston's conceptual scheme, what happens if I change my mind about the worth of what I am doing is that I perform a further elicited act of will, which in its turn impresses another impetus upon the body, and the second impetus duly has an effect upon the movement of the body, an effect which is itself affected in part by the impetus previously impressed. The situation was familiar to medieval philosophers speculating about physics – they knew that a projectile could be deflected by another projectile. The impetus impressed by the second projectile did not simply annihilate the impetus in the first one. Instead the subsequent course of the projectile was a product of the first impetus and the second. Likewise if I am running north and decide to run west, I cannot straightaway run west; even the most abrupt change in direction is modified by the previous action.

Thus the fact that I have performed an elicited act of will has not thereby prevented any further free act till the commanded act has duly run its course. I am free to change the act by imparting a further impetus. Naturally I am not so free that I can change course as if I had not previously been set upon a course, but in any case nobody supposes that we are so free that we can enter upon a course of action without in any way being restricted by our point of departure.

While recognising there are limits to the kinds of things we are free to do and therefore to make of ourselves, a great many details have to be filled in regarding where those limits are. In this connection Manderston raises a variety of points. In our discussion of his philosophy of action we began by noting that virtues are dispositions of will. Freedom stands in an interesting relation to the kind of disposition that is classed as a virtue. It is by acting as we do that our virtues are formed; by repeatedly imitating the just person we might eventually become just; by repeatedly imitating the courageous person we might eventually become courageous, and so on. The repetitious acts are themselves willed, and hence the dispositions are products of acts of will. Nevertheless a distinction has to be drawn here, for though the acts by which a disposition is formed are free it does not follow that the formation of the disposition by the performance of those free acts is itself free.[61] It was Manderston's view that the formation of the disposition is due to natural causation even in the case where a person performs the free acts precisely in order that the disposition may be formed. In this respect the situation is no different from the case where a person develops muscles by repeated physical exercise. The muscle development is a natural causal consequence of the exercise, even though the exercising is free.

However, though there is a natural causal explanation for the production of a disposition, the acts which are embodiments of the disposition are themselves free. Thus though the courageous disposition is a natural consequence of repeated imitations of a courageous man, the acts which are performed once the courageous disposition has been formed are free. The naturalness of the production of a disposition is expressed by Manderston even at the level of definition. He defines 'disposition' as 'a quality in a cognitive power, naturally produced by an act or acts, with the quality remaining in the power when the acts have ceased, and inclining the agent immediately to similar acts [viz. acts similar to the ones which produced that cognitive quality]'.[62] Manderston explains his position by saying that we will acts of a certain kind, and by nature, not will, we develop a disposition to perform such acts. The will, he tells us, does not cooperate in the formation of the disposition, though all acts produced by the disposition are produced with the cooperation of the will.

An essential aspect of this account is that while it is acts in imitation of a virtuous person's behaviour which produce acts which are virtuous, it does not follows that every act produced by a given disposition is of the same species as the act by which the disposition is produced. Manderston employs an important distinction here: a disposition can incline, or 'dispose', us mediately or immediately.

A disposition inclines us immediately to produce an act like the act which caused the formation of the disposition – as, for example, a courageous disposition, formed by courageous acts, disposes us immediately to act courageously. And mediately it disposes us to perform an act which removes an impediment to the act which we are immediately disposed to perform; for example, the soldier's courage leads him to check his weapons as well as to use them.[63]

Whether the commanded act is an immediate act of virtue or mediates between the disposition and the act of virtue, the obvious thing to say is that the act is free. But a question can be raised as to whether there could be a disposition so intense or a passion so vehement that the will is necessitated to conform to that disposition or passion.[64] For the will to be necessitated, Manderston explains, is 'for someone to receive or produce in himself an act from which he cannot freely desist'. The disjunction 'receive or produce' is presumably used here to indicate a role for the agent which is less than that implied by 'produce' alone; where an agent performs an act from which he cannot freely desist it would be as true to say that he receives or even 'undergoes' the act as to say that he produces it.

The damned cannot freely desist from enduring their punishment. They are eternally trapped in it, and likewise the blessed cannot freely desist from their enjoyment of the beatific vision. These examples are chosen by Manderston because the damned and the blessed are enduring or enjoying their recompense in accordance with the irreversible ordination of God. The irredeemability of the damned is the source of the necessitation of their will. This situation contrasts with that of the wayfarer, the person on his pilgrimage through this life, whose will is, in general, not necessitated since he remains free to do good or evil. It is not in doubt that God can give us a spiritual push in the direction of the good, but such a push, though having persuasive force, does not necessitate the will. Manderston's picture of the wayfarer is, therefore, of a person whose future state is not yet determined. By an act of full contrition, or by a refusal to repent, he contributes to the determination of his future state. The point here is that Manderston likens our dispositions and passions to the spiritual push by which God puts pressure on our will. That pressure falls short of necessitation. Similarly our dispositions and passions, however strong or vehement, can at most be persuasive but cannot by any means necessitate our will.

Hence Manderston must reject the concept of an ungovernable rage which pitches us into action contrary to will. It is not just that, however vehement the passion, we can always distance ourselves sufficiently to give the will a chance to perform an elicited act. The point is that that is what always happens. The passion might be so intense as to be highly persuasive in its urgings; but there is always a question as to whether the will is in fact going to yield to those urgings. And if it yields then the resulting action, the commanded action, is no less willed than if the passion had been calm. Manderston mentions temptation in this context. If it is vehement the agent might yield to it, then say that he acted unwillingly, would rather not have yielded, but the temptation was too strong. However, to say that the act was performed unwillingly is to say, not that the act was not willed, but that it was regretted even while it was being performed. Since the act, however pressing the temptation, was willed, the agent was not caught helpless in the trap of temptation as the damned are trapped in hell. In just the same way we are not trapped in our dispositions and passions. By contrast, with all the power of their being, the damned can say 'no' to their punishment, but their dissent might as well not exist for all the difference it makes to what they seek to reject.

Hence acting under the influence of a passion does not imply that the act is not free, and would not imply it even if it were added that the passion is intense. Likewise with actions performed on the basis of a disposition. Indeed, we should keep a firm grasp of the fact that dispositions merely *dispose* us to act, they do not push us or frogmarch us into an act. On the contrary, if all we know about a given person is that he is disposed to perform act A, we do not know whether he will perform it or not. Of course we might say that he is more likely to perform it, but to know that he is more likely to is not to know what he will in fact do. Furthermore, we recognise that a person may have a disposition to perform a given act yet either not perform it ever or not perform it for a long period during which he has the disposition. But if the act follows from a disposition as an effect follows by nature from its cause, then why is it that the effect happens at one time rather than another? And how can the effect possibly not occur if the cause is in place?

Thus the fact that a person has a disposition to perform acts of a given kind still leaves room for an exercise of will. In fact it leaves all the room in the world since the person can face the disposition and still say 'no' to it, however strong it may be. But it does not follow, and neither did Manderston think it might follow, that the presence of the disposition makes no difference to what the agent wills to do. To say it made no difference would be to say that the agent did not after all have the disposition. One might say that the existence of the disposition does have an effect in that it determines the form of the practical question that the agent asks himself. Since he has a disposition to do A, the performance of A is, so to say, his default position, and what he asks himself is whether there is an overriding reason not to do A, that is, a reason which overrides (among other things) the disposition.

What has just been said about dispositions can be said also about passions. It is true that passions do not compel or necessitate the will, but they can still have an effect in so far as they determine the agent's default position. Thus, having a strong passion which dictates that the agent do A, his question to himself is this: is there an overriding reason why I should not do A, that is, a reason which overrides (among other things) that passion? Hence the fact that the agent is free not to act in the direction dictated by his passion, does not imply that the passion does not have an effect on the shape of the agent's behaviour.

The opposite point can also be made, and Manderston duly makes it. We have already observed that Manderston holds that the will is the place of virtue or, as he also puts it, virtue, in its subjective aspect, should be placed in the faculty of will. He uses the phrase 'in its subjective aspect' in order to indicate that he is thinking of virtue as a quality of the soul, rather than as a visible pattern of virtuous behaviour. Given the place of virtue, as in the will, it follows that an agent cannot act virtuously except by will, that is, every expression of the virtuous disposition must be an expression of the will.

One such expression of that disposition which Manderston stresses is the curbing or moderating of the passions. Or more precisely, he held that the virtuous disposition expresses itself in the curbing of those passions which obstruct the realisation of the goals of right reason, and in the promoting of those passions which further those goals. Thus it is Manderston's view that just as the passions can have an effect on the will, so the will can have an effect on the passions not only in the sense that the will can control the passions by willing actions which are contrary to those passions, but also in the sense that it can control the passions by moderating their strength or intensity, or by increasing that strength or intensity. Thus not only can a virtuous person feel very angry without acting as the anger dictates, he can also moderate the anger so that its presence is less of an obstacle than it would have been to action conformable with right reason.

There are deep things here. I suggested earlier that passion can set the agenda, leaving it to the will to determine whether to act as passion dictates. Will can say 'no', but nevertheless, as Manderston observes, passion can still give the will more work to do; it can be an obstacle even if one that is never insurmountable. But if the will can moderate, or strengthen, a passion, it follows that passion may not after all set the agenda. The goal of the virtuous person is to perform only acts which are conformable with right reason. In the interests of doing this it can so affect a given passion that it ceases to be the dominant voice among the passions. It is common enough for there to be several passions pulling in opposite directions. The strongest of these sets the agenda. If the will can moderate that passion sufficiently it will no longer be the dominant one, that is, the one setting the agenda; thus as a result of the act of will the strongest passion is one which dictates a line of action which is as a matter of fact in conformity with the line dictated by right reason. Hence the will can work on and through the passions to secure the goal of reason. To a certain extent therefore a passion can be thought of as having much the same status as a commanded act [*actus imperatus*], for to a certain extent the passion is a product of the will. Perhaps the will does not produce the passion where there had previously not been one, but it may greatly contribute to the determination of the shape and strength of a passion which is already in existence.

If passion is to a certain extent under the dominion of the will, can the same be said for belief? We have already taken note of this question in the course of our examination of the writings of Ireland, and of certain members of Mair's circle. I should like now to revert to this central question and look at it through the eyes of Manderston. Later we shall consider David Hume's response to the question, and Manderston's answer will help us to see more clearly how we should respond to Hume's discussion of the same topic.

Manderston has to deal with this problem because he faces up to an argument which, if sound, shows that some meritorious acts are non-free. The premisses of the argument are: (1) every act of believing is a non-free act, and (2) some acts of believing are meritorious.[65] It is the first of these premisses, the major premiss, which concerns us for the present. In its favour it might be argued that it is contrary to experience that the will can make the understanding assent to any proposition, but that argument implies that the will does not cooperate in the believing in articles of faith. The Oxford Dominican, Robert Holkot, expounded this heterodox opinion at the start of his Commentary on the *Sentences of Peter Lombard*. Holkot's thesis was that every act of believing is purely natural and is caused purely naturally by motives which necessitate the understanding.

In illustration of Holkot's thesis, I can argue as follows: I believe that there is a sheet of paper on the desk before me. I believe this because I can see the sheet on the desk; the will can play no role here. I can say it is not there, or even entertain a sceptical metaphysician's doubt about its presence, but all the same, even if I do either of these things, I am not going to look elsewhere for paper to write on nor am I going to give as my reason the fact that I have willed not to believe in the presentness to me of this sheet of paper which I see to be on the desk as plainly as I can see anything anywhere. The strength of Holkot's position is obvious.

Yet Manderston thinks Holkot's thesis is wrong about this, and he brings two arguments to bear. First, only what can be brought under the will can be commanded, but God commands us to believe; hence believing can be subordinated to the will.[66] This argument does not establish, or seek to establish, that all believing is subordinate to the will. It establishes only that believing which is commanded by God can be subordinate. But even this more limited claim is, if correct, sufficient to undermine Holkot's thesis.

Manderston's second argument is this: if the act of believing were purely natural and effected by causes which necessitate the understanding, then an act of unbelief [*infidelitas*] should not be called unmeritorious.[67] This argument relies upon the unstated premiss that an act which cannot be willed should not be judged unmeritorious. Hence, if we could not do otherwise, we should not be blamed or punished for our act. On this concept of merit we can earn merit by our free acts. This concept, which has semi-pelagian overtones, is certainly not the only concept of merit, and in particular it contrasts with the concept of merit as an absolutely free acceptance, by God, of a person for eternal reward. This is an important matter historically as well as theologically, since the theology of good works was one of the chief battlegrounds of the Reformation. However, each side in this dispute might hold that an act of unbelief could be seen as a proof of demerit, whether or not the act was itself subject to the will.

Of the two positions given above, Holkot's and its contrary, Manderston judges that the second is likelier, though he does so at least as much on the basis of scriptural warrant as on the basis of philosophical argument. However, Holkot was a very distinguished protagonist on the theological stage, and Manderston was reluctant simply to dismiss his view. He preferred to take the line that there was some truth in the doctrine of Holkot, even if it was less than the whole truth.

In support of this approach Manderston invokes a distinction we have already dealt with at length, that between evident and inevident assent. The evidence for some propositions is so great as to leave no room for the will to play a role. For example, I have only to look at the desk in front of me to see that there is a sheet of paper on it. But not all assent is evident. Often, as we have noted, when the evidence is not so great as to leave no room for doubt, we assent but are not compelled to by the weight of evidence. Such assent, inevident assent, cannot be given without an act of will.[68] We can therefore hold, as Manderston does, that certain propositions which may be evident in themselves, are not evident to us, even though there is some evidence for them. They are however presented to us on the authority of another person, and we decide to take his word for the truth of the propositions. In taking that decision our will is immediately engaged. If, on that basis, we believe, we believe by an act of will. But we can still allow that Holkot is correct in saying that believing is purely natural and is caused by purely natural motives which necessitate the understanding, so long as we take him to be speaking about assent to, and therefore belief in, evident propositions.

This is not to say that the will cannot play a role even of a mediate sort in evident assent, for we can by will direct our attention to something to which we thereupon give evident assent. In such a case the will plays some part in the production of the assent. Manderston's point however is untouched by that consideration, for his claim is that the will, whether or not it can produce evident assent mediately, cannot produce it immediately. If he is right about this it follows that evident assent is an act that has no moral value. But inevident assent is quite differently placed in relation to moral valuation, precisely because such assent is subordinate to the will, and is therefore no less available for moral assessment than is any other willed act.

Perhaps the most important consideration in respect of moral assessment is the object intended. Manderston writes: 'The absolutely ultimate end of all good human acts should be God Himself, so that no act is morally good unless it is done ultimately for the sake of God.'[69] This is not to say that nothing else has to be taken into consideration in determining the moral worth of an act. For example, the means adopted to secure the end must also be good. On this matter Manderston registers his disagreement with St Thomas Aquinas who held that an act is good-and-bad if it is a morally bad means for the sake of a good end. Manderston's example is of a theft which is committed to help a pauper for the sake of God, an act which Manderston describes as entirely false and erroneous.[70] He defends his judgement on this matter by pointing out that more things are required for an act to be good than are required for it not to be good. We need not pursue the details which lie behind this defence, but shall merely note the position, and keep it in mind as we take up the point that he identifies God as the ultimate end of morally good acts. The issue provides a link with Manderston's teaching on grace, which I wish to address.

That all morally good acts are done ultimately for the sake of God, is a claim that has at first blush an intolerant air, for surely it implies that only those who accept the revealed God (particularly those who accept the God of the Trinity) are morally good. And in that case those who are guided by the light of nature, and not by a supernatural light, are not morally good. Manderston offers this line of thought as worthy of consideration, and then proceeds to attack both the opinion and also, and just as importantly, the attitude it represents. It is Manderston's view that there have been philosophers who have been guided solely by the light of nature and who have in no way been vouchsafed a divine revelation, who have nevertheless learned a great deal about God. Among their discoveries, according to Manderston, are the facts that there is 'a highest being, who is supremely good and supremely perfect, ruler of all things, upon whom depend all goodness and perfection, and who gives being to all things'.[71] These facts about the highest being, he adds, are sufficient to persuade us that the highest being should be loved for His own sake. The conclusion that Manderston draws is that 'it is false that to be morally good an act must be done for the sake of the Father, or of the Son, or of the Holy Spirit'. It is enough that it be done for the sake of God as He is known to us by the light of nature.

However, this position, a comparatively tolerant one, requires defence against attack from within the Church, for it appears to be in conflict with a central teaching on the role of grace in the moral life. Manderston, following a traditional doctrine, describes grace as 'a quality infused by God as a sign of His love of a rational being, with which quality every good act performed in this life merits beatitude'.[72] This is the realist concept of grace, firmly established in Christian theology by St Thomas Aquinas. It is distinguished by its Aristotelian overtone of a disposition in the soul; though whereas Aristotle spoke of dispositions produced in a person's soul by his own efforts, Aquinas spoke of grace as infused in the soul by a free act of God. But as well as this dispositional concept of grace there is another concept, one we have already met with, namely special grace, a concept found in the 'prince of Thomists', John Capreol, whose significance is therefore not uniform for nominalists and realists. Several Scottish writers attended to the concept, including Manderston, who payed close attention to it, as did his colleagues George Lokert and John Mair. The concept also emerges in the writings of the makars. In *The Prais of Aige*, Robert Henryson writes:

> The stait of yowth I reput for na gude,
> for in that stait sic perrel now I se;
> but* speciall grace, the regeing of his blude [*without]
> can nane ganestand quhill that he aigit be.[73]

John Ireland tells us in *The Mirror of Wisdom* that he had written a book 'proving that the help and support of God, that is called *speciale auxilium* [special help] . . . is necessary to evade and eschew sin, and that we may not through our proper virtue do works of merit. And this is a high and great matter in theology, for the same singular and special help of God and grace is necessary to all merit and good works.'[74]

This concept is duly inherited by Manderston who adds clarification. He tells us that special grace is a help by which God, preceding our will, moves it to produce a good act.[75] Manderston also describes it as an internal push [*impulsus interior*] or a special motion which moves the will.[76] Such terminology suggests that Manderston is not thinking of special grace in accordance with St Thomas Aquinas's account, for that account is of grace considered as a disposition, whereas Manderston is evidently thinking of special grace as something episodic.

One may speculate about how determinative of human action special grace is. As regards Manderston's position on that matter he nowhere suggests that special grace is irresistible. Nor would we expect him to, for his general position, which is thoroughly Thomist, is that our will cannot be compelled or forced even by God – for the will is by its nature the faculty of freedom. It could not be forced without its nature first being destroyed, in which case it would not be the will which acted under compulsion, but some other faculty which replaced it and was essentially different from it. Hence where we are truly determined, the will plays no part whatever. We should recall here that Robert Henryson speaks of special grace as if it were a necessary condition for virtuous action, but not a sufficient condition. Without special grace youth cannot control its passions. Henryson implies that with such grace it can do so, but not that it will. Similarly John Ireland speaks of special grace as necessary if we are to eschew sin, but he does not suggest that with special grace we will succeed. Even an act performed under an impulse from special grace might be sinful.

On this matter Manderston invokes the fourteenth-century master Gregory of Rimini.[77] In his *Commentary on the Sentences of Peter Lombard* Bk II, Gregory, addressing theologians, lays down two crucial propositions: (1) without God's special help in addition to dispositional grace, a person cannot have sufficient knowledge of what ought to be done; (2) even with sufficient knowledge of what ought to be done, we cannot in this life produce a morally good act without the special help of God. Gregory states that the cause of this weakness is original sin, by which we are so immersed in and united to sensuality that without an inner impulse from God we could never rise above our sensuality and perform a good act.

I do not think that John Ireland would disagree with Gregory's position, but Manderston certainly does, as he signals by referring to Gregory's position as a *fantasia*. In place of that *fantasia* Manderston commends a 'common opinion' according to which 'a person's free will can produce an act which is morally entirely good without God's special help, though it could not produce a meritorious *act* [that is, an act meritorious of eternal life] without the special help and grace of God'.

Manderston is anxious to guard against misunderstanding on this matter. In line with his conception of the will as the faculty of freedom, he holds that a meritorious *act* is immediately within the free power of a person; what is not in his free power is that the act be meritorious. There is no act of merit except one done in a state of absolutely freely given grace.

Given this point, we can now ask whether a person can indeed, as Manderston says, produce a morally entirely good act without God's special help. In line with standard medieval practice, let us take the acts commanded by God as our examples of morally entirely good acts. Our question now becomes this: can we freely will to fulfill the commands of God? Manderston is well aware that some authoritative texts answer that question in the negative, and he is plainly uneasy about that fact, though reluctant to say so. Instead he does what every medieval philosopher did in that situation – he makes a distinction. We can understand the phrase 'fulfill the commands of God' in two ways.[78] (1) An act may not only accord with a divine command but also be accompanied by God's intention that the agent be rewarded with eternal life. (2) An act can accord with a command of God where the act is not accompanied by such an intention. If an act fulfills a command of God, in the first sense of that phrase, it must be done by special grace. On this view the authoritative texts are correct. But an act can fulfill the commands of God, in the second sense of the phrase, without requiring God's special grace. Manderston makes it plain that his sympathies lie with the linguistic practice embodied in the second sense listed above of 'fulfill the commands of God'. He wishes to say that our will is by itself, that is, without a special act of God, sufficient to produce not only a morally bad act but also a morally good one. Manderston thus places the full weight of responsibility upon our free will.

We have now identified two distinct aspects of special grace. First, it is an impulse or push by God which puts pressure, albeit resistible pressure, on our will; and secondly, it involves a divine intention to accept a willed act as meriting eternal reward. If emphasis is placed on the second aspect, and there is reason to place it just there, the concept of special grace has a distinctly nominalist ring to it, for special grace would be understood as God's acceptance of an action as meriting a reward for the agent. Thus, in so far as a person receives an impulse of special grace his nature is not thereby changed. He remains a fallen human being, naturally concupiscent, unable to save himself by his own efforts, however capable he may be of producing, by an elicited act of will, morally good acts. This concept of grace is far from the realist concept developed by St Thomas Aquinas, according to which grace, as a disposition of the soul, cannot be acquired by the agent without his nature thereby being changed. The infusion of grace makes the agent a new person; it effects a rebirth.

I began this chapter with some remarks about Manderston's pupil Patrick Hamilton, theologian and proto-martyr of the Scottish Reformation, and should like to end with some comments which I hope will indicate possible lines of research on the relation between Mair's circle and Patrick Hamilton.

In Hamilton's little treatise *Patrick's Place* we hear a voice which is very different from Manderston's. Manderston's is the voice of the medieval schoolman. It is calm, reasonable, developing arguments in a systematic fashion, with close attention to the logical details – and here we should remember that Manderston, who wrote a lengthy treatise on logic, was one of the foremost logicians of his generation. *Patrick's Places*, on the other hand, is sharply insistent and the arguments are far less detailed. Nevertheless the impact of the little treatise is great.

The main topic is grace and its relation to morality. Hamilton addresses the question, which so interested Manderston, of whether a morally good act can be performed without grace, and his argument is luminously clear: He who has faith loves God, he who loves God loves his neighbour, he who loves his neighbour keeps all the commandments of God. Therefore he who has faith keeps all the commandments of God. It is by grace of God that we have faith in Him. Therefore it is by grace of God that we keep His commandments. The commandments articulate moral goodness. Therefore it is by grace of God that we are morally good.[79] Grace is not in our power. Therefore it is not in our power to be morally good.

This line of argument, which in its essentials is not new, bears a close resemblance to the position of Gregory of Rimini which we considered earlier. The main difference is that Gregory holds that special grace is required for the performance of a morally good act, and Hamilton holds that what is required is faith by God's grace. Manderston could therefore reply to Hamilton by invoking his distinction between performing a morally good act, which is in our power, and performing a meritorious one, which, in respect of its merit, is not. However Manderston accepts the standard doctrine that every human act, and therefore every good one also, requires God's general cooperation; God's ordering of the circumstances of our actions has an effect both on the content of our elicited acts and on the realisation or otherwise of the commanded acts. We might therefore hold that Hamilton is on the same side as Gregory or on the same side as Manderston, for Manderston, while stressing that by our unaided efforts we can do good, does not suppose that by our unaided efforts we can save ourselves.

While it is appropriate to notice similarities, it is however a mistake not to stress the differences. Historically the differences proved more important. Hamilton asserts: 'The law biddeth us do that which is impossible for us'. He then asks: 'Wherefore doth God command that which is impossible for us?'. And his answer is that God's command reveals to us our evil, and also reveals to us that we can seek a remedy only at the hands of another.

Manderston's position is more humane. He bids us remember that we are commanded to love our neighbour, and that we can obey that command by our own efforts. And also, we can, by our own efforts, demonstrate the existence of a perfect being, ruler of all, through love of whom we should love our neighbour. Hence not only is the act sound; so also is the motive. It is easier to warm to Manderston than to Hamilton, but in many ways Hamilton better represented the ethos of his age than did Manderston. The world was rapidly changing into one in which Manderston could not easily have felt at home. In the next chapter I shall turn to a consideration of some aspects of the philosophy of that new age.

7 The Post-Medieval Period

John Mair and his circle lived at a time of great change, a change apparent in a wide range of cultural activities including the writing of academic books. A glance at the books of Mair's circle tells us that those men belonged to the old order. They were all logicians and the logic dictated the way they wrote. They could hardly say anything without producing an argument in justification, and they would then offer objections to the original thesis or to the supporting arguments. The objections in their turn would be subjected to logical scrutiny. And so the process would continue until the writers were sure that the original thesis was as firmly supported as it humanly could be. They would then proceed to the next thesis, and treat it in exactly the same way. Needless to say most of their treatises were long. But that was not thought an objection to them; on the contrary, since it was recognised that the truth was often difficult and complex, any purported attempt at a brief exposition of the truth would have been regarded with suspicion. If an inherently complex matter is presented as if it were simple the presentation must be false.

Another feature of the writings of Mair's circle that should be noted is the Latin style. It was the style of the schoolmen, and though possessing its own beauty and having its own standard of excellence, it was very far removed from the language of Cicero and Virgil out of which it developed over the centuries. But this feature of the language of philosophy was under threat. In sixteenth-century Scotland the classical Roman authors began to be studied in earnest, and Greek also was placed on the agenda by men who were tough enough to brave the hostility of a segment of the Church which appeared to believe that its interpretation of the New Testament, based upon the Vulgate edition, would be threatened if people could read the New Testament in Greek. As part of the change, for the first time in Scotland Plato and Aristotle were being read in Greek. Soon the academic scene was transformed. The start of the sixteenth century found Scotland almost totally lacking in Greek scholars, but by the end of that century the first principal of Edinburgh University, the theologian Robert Rollock, was, to nobody's surprise or alarm, using the original Greek texts in his lectures on logic. Indeed, as mentioned earlier, there is contemporary evidence that those lectures to his undergraduates consisted of hardly more than a dictating of the recently edited Greek texts. This would have been unthinkable in Mair's day.

The change was in part the product of a change in aesthetic standards. People reading the great authors of classical Rome were bowled over by their linguistic styles and if you are enthralled with an author's style you are likely to imitate it. Cicero became the stylistic role model for many sixteenth-century philosophers (and not only philosophers). One does not require to read much philosophy by Scottish writers in the middle of the century to realise that the Renaissance had truly arrived in the country. It came to Scotland later than to most other countries in western Europe, but when it arrived its impact was no less dramatic. The language of the Scottish authors is a clear sign of the revolution. The style is frequently, if self-consciously, Ciceronian, and where Greek philosophers are quoted, it was normal to quote them in Greek. In some respects Mair and David Cranston were pioneers in this change in so far as they attended the lectures on Greek which, despite the nervousness of the Faculty of Theology, Girolamo Aleandro delivered in the University of Paris.[80] Indeed Mair slipped a number of Greek terms into his last book, his Commentary on the *Nicomachean Ethics* published in 1530.

The stylish Latin of the new writings on philosophy was not pure gain. Even if the sixteenth-century humanists despised the Latin of the preceding generations of schoolmen and thought it barbaric, it had a great deal to be said for it, including a great deal about which many humanists could know only little. The schoolmen used their Latin creatively in response to their desire to say things with the utmost clarity. They developed rules concerning word order, where the important consideration was the signification of the terms, given the order in which they appear in the proposition. In a sense they were engaged in the massive project of developing a scientific Latin, and in that project rhetorical flourishes and beautiful turns of phrase were simply an irrelevance. The only thing that the schoolmen were interested in was the unambiguously expressed truth. For example, the rule which permitted them to distinguish between 'Every man has a head' and 'A head every man has' is one which is of great use to philosophers, and has been rediscovered (and promptly employed by philosophers) in the last hundred years. Thus for example some have thought that Aristotle reveals a failure to make just that sort of distinction when he slides from 'Everything aims at some good' to 'There is some good at which everything aims'.[81]

Humanists mocked the examples given by the logicians and were highly critical of the enormous number of logical rules, 'these waggon-loads of trifles' as Melanchthon called them. And it might indeed be argued that in a sense medieval logic, whose final glorious flowering came with the circle of John Mair in the early sixteenth century, in the end collapsed under its own weight, the sheer weight of rules invented to deal with the countless cases which came up. It is easy to understand the frustration of the American philosopher C. S. Pierce when he complained about the 'damnable particularity' of medieval logic, but at the same time his criticism misses the point, which is that the logicians were concerned to show us how to argue logically in a non-artificial language, and there is no reason in principle why the list of rules required for that should be limited, and even less is there reason for supposing the total number of rules to be small.

Human language has a magical power to present us with inferences whose validity cannot be demonstrated without recourse to rules of valid inference which nobody had thought to formulate. Sometimes, also, inferences which look as though they are valid turn out not to be valid after all if accepted rules are applied. In that case logicians have either to offer refinements of those earlier rules, or to offer analyses of the dubious inferences which show that they are after all invalid, and are not exemplifications of the rules of valid inference. Thus to take two sample inferences: 'The more you are ugly the more you adorn yourself, and the more you adorn yourself the more you are beautiful; therefore the more you are ugly the more you are beautiful', and 'If I say that you are a donkey I say that you are an animal, and if I say that you are an animal I say the truth [since man is a rational animal]; therefore if I say that you are a donkey I say the truth', both raised problems which were within the purview of medieval logicians.[82] These were the kinds of case which called for a close analysis of language, and it was as logicians that the medieval philosophers entered upon such analyses.

Medieval logicians fully appreciated the endless resource-fulness of human language, perhaps more than many modern logicians do, and they regarded their lists of rules as, so to say, a holding operation till the next problem presented itself and had to be dealt with in turn. With the arrival of the humanist revolution there was a dramatic change. Two things happened, and Scottish philosophers were to the fore in both develop-ments. The first was a return to an ancient view of logic as a subsidiary art to rhetoric, the art of persuasion. This in turn led to a close analysis of language, but from the point of view of the grammarian rather than of the logician. Thus the logic textbooks with their endless rules of valid inference were gradually replaced in the curricula of universities by textbooks listing and discussing parts of speech. By an ironic turn of events, the lists of parts of speech became steadily longer and, by the end of the century, large textbooks of grammar and rhetoric came to be no less crammed with rules of parts of speech than the logic textbooks had been with rules of valid inference.

The second thing that happened is one I have already signalled by my reference, at the start of this chapter, to Robert Rollock's lectures. It was the return to Aristotle. But the phrase 'return to Aristotle' requires explanation. In substantial measure the logic, metaphysics, epistemology, and ethics, of the medieval thinkers at least from the middle of the thirteenth century were a commentary upon Aristotle. The works of Aristotle were by then becoming readily available in Latin translations, and Christian thinkers, recognising deep truths in the writings of a 'pagan' thinker, recognised also that it was essential to square their own Christian philosophical and theological speculations with Aristotle's system. Much of what they wrote thereafter was in the form of Commentaries upon Aristotle, and even where it was not explicitly in that form, it was easy to see Aristotle's long shadow. The process can fairly be described as the Christianisation of Aristotle. It is not to be wondered at that medieval philosophers referred to Aristotle simply as *philosophus*, 'the philosopher'. As already mentioned, Mair's last book was a Commentary on one of Aristotle's ethical works. In the light of all this, my phrase 'the return to Aristotle', used of the humanist revolution, certainly requires explanation.

The explanation is that by the early sixteenth century it was very difficult to read the real Aristotle under the accretions of several centuries of commentaries. There are two aspects to this. First, the medieval commentaries were on Latin translations, not on the original Greek writings. Secondly it was difficult even to think about Aristotle except in terms of the categories, definitions, and distinctions which were introduced by the medievals. What was required was an abandonment of the whole medieval logical and philosophical enterprise in so far as that was oriented towards Aristotle; which, in its turn, required the abandonment of the logic and philosophy of the Middle Ages. What was called for was a fresh start with the Greek texts of Aristotle, properly edited, and shorn of their medieval accretions. The Christianisation of Aristotle was thought to have been carried quite far enough, indeed too far, since the brilliant light cast by the original texts had all but been snuffed out by the remorseless activity of the commentators.

From the point of view of the students this change had at least one desirable effect; it meant that far fewer rules of valid inference needed to be learned. Teachers restricted themselves in large measure to dictating the Greek text and to expounding it in such a way as to avoid regression into the supposedly bad old ways of doing logic which characterised their scholastic predecessors. The situation was the same in other areas of philosophy also.

In Scotland the change came suddenly. An example of it is provided by William Cranston (no relation, so far as is known, of David Cranston of whom we have already spoken). William Cranston had been rector of the University of Paris before returning to Scotland, to St Andrews, where in due course he succeeded John Mair as provost of St Salvator's College. He was a friend of George Buchanan and would play a dominant role in Scottish academic life. In 1540 he dedicated to David Beaton, Cardinal Archbishop of St Andrews, a book *Dialecticae compendium* [*A Compendium of Logic*] which was only seven folios long. In it he presents logic in the form of a diagram. It had been common practice among medieval logicians to include logic diagrams in their textbooks, but they did not think that they could say it all in a diagram, even less that they could do so in as meagre a diagram as the one William Cranston presented.

At the start of the *Compendium* we are told, diagrammatically, that a term is a subject or predicate of a proposition, and that it can 'usefully' be classified under one or another of only five headings. The five are as follows: (1) univocal or equivocal (that is, having just one meaning, or having more than one); (2) material or personal (that is, roughly, signifying itself, as the term 'man' does in ' "Man" is a monosyllable', or signifying what it customarily signifies, as 'man' does in 'Peter is a man'); (3) connotative or absolute (that is, either (a) signifying one thing primarily and another secondarily, as 'white' primarily signifies a white thing and secondarily signifies whiteness, or (b) not signifying both primarily and secondarily, for example, 'animal', which signifies cattle, donkeys, and so on, and does not signify anything else in a secondary way); (4) common or singular (that is, fitted by its nature to signify just one thing, or fitted to signify several things); and (5) name of a noun or name of a thing (for example, 'noun' in contrast to 'dog').

Cranston adds that he omits all other divisions and definitions because they are of little use to philosophers. In the light of the immense advances made by logicians in the preceding few centuries, this is a truly extraordinary claim, especially coming from a man who not only knew Mair and members of his circle, but had been brought up on the immensely powerful logic which those men had done so much to advance. For example, William Cranston does not even list the distinction between categorematic and syncategorematic terms, which enabled logicians to distinguish between terms which signify things, and terms, such as 'every', 'some', 'no', 'and', 'or', and 'if', in other words, all the terms in which logicians are interested. William Cranston also fails to mention supposition, though many of the valuable advances made by logicians in the medieval period had been made in connection with their theory of supposition.

In large measure Cranston's *Compendium* involves a return to the *Organon*, the collection of logical works by Aristotle. But not entirely. A conspicuous example is the brief mention he makes of the so-called 'hypothetical syllogism'. This is an inference in which at least one of the premisses contains a complex proposition, that is, one composed of two propositions linked by 'and', 'or', or 'if'. For example 'Jack is tall or Jill is short, and Jack is not tall; therefore Jill is short' and 'If Jack is hungry Jill feeds him, and Jill does not feed him; therefore Jack is not hungry' are both hypothetical syllogisms. Inferences of this sort are not discussed by Aristotle, though later writers, for example, Boethius, made a detailed study of them. In the first edition of the *Compendium* there is no reference to those later logicians, but in the second edition (published 1545) Cranston states both that Aristotle did not discuss hypothetical syllogisms, and also that he, Cranston, is basing his remarks on the subject on Boethius.

The reference to Boethius is not the only respect in which the second edition differs from the first. Another, and more conspicuous, difference is the length of the second edition. Evidently Cranston decided that the brevity of his first edition was a drawback for the students for whom he had written the work; they needed more exposition of his definitions and distinctions and they needed illustrations also. The result of this change of heart was a much more discursive edition in 1545 than he had been prepared to offer in 1540 when he clearly regarded the sheer brevity of his exposition as a virtue.

Once he starts to talk in sentences rather than diagrams it becomes evident that William Cranston has not quite discarded his medieval heritage. I shall restrict myself to one example of this. In the second edition, before the first diagram, Cranston distinguishes between grammarians and logicians. The two groups attend to language, but they do not classify language in the same way. For the grammarian there are four levels of complexity, viz. letters, syllables, words [*dictiones*], and propositions [*orationes*]. For the logician there are three levels, viz.

terms, propositions, and inferences. Letters and syllables are, as such, irrelevant to the logician. I say 'as such' because if a single letter or a single syllable forms a word, as does, for example, 'I' or 'cat' then the logician is indeed interested in them, but that is because they form words, not because they consist of a single letter or a single syllable. Cranston does not specify the basis of his distinction between the things in which the logician and the grammarian are respectively interested. Nevertheless from the little he says on this matter it is clear that he is relying on the doctrine that logicians are concerned with a piece of language only so far as it has signification, and grammarians are not. Thus the minimum linguistic unit with which the logician is concerned is a piece of language (1) which has signification and (2) of which no part has a signification which contributes to the signification of the whole piece. For example, the term 'singular' contains 'sin' as a part. 'Sin' has signification, but the signification of 'sin' in no way contributes to the signification of 'singular' for someone who is unclear as to the signification of 'singular' would not be helped by being told what 'sin' stands for. A grammarian, on the other hand, is interested in the fact that a part of a given term is a syllable, even though the syllable has no signification, or has a signification which does not contribute to the signification of the whole. These matters were worked out by, among others, William Cranston's namesake David Cranston. It is interesting to see this thoroughly scholastic theory breaking through the humanist efforts of a man who is trying to present himself as belonging to the new order.

His wish to associate himself with the new order is clear from the sources he quotes. He makes several references to Porphyry (*c.*AD232–305, author of an influential introduction to the *Categories* of Aristotle), quotes Cicero, and, of special significance in this connection, invokes Rudolph Agricola, the great humanist from the Netherlands, as for example when Cranston criticises logicians who confuse logical division (such as the division of animal into rational and non-rational) with partition (for example the partition of animal into head, body, etc). The chief logical difference between these two kinds of case is that as regards logical division the more general term is truly predicable of the less general ones (for example, a rational animal is an animal and so is a non-rational one). But as regards partition, the greater term is not predicable of the lesser ones (for example, a head is not an animal, and neither is a body). It is in this connection that Cranston refers to Cicero's statement in his *Topics* that a whole is unlike a genus, for a whole cannot be affirmed of any part taken individually, whereas a genus can be affirmed of any member of a species falling under that genus (for example, since the species 'cat' falls under the genus 'animal', the cat Tibbles must be an animal). The notable thing here is that Cranston supports his position by reference to that handbook of the humanists, Rudolph Agricola's *De inventione dialectica*.

The very title of Agricola's book reveals the humanist pre-dilections of its author. It means 'Concerning logical discovery'. The discovery in question is of persuasive premises for the thesis the speaker wishes to persuade others to accept. The main logical concern of the logicians who formed Mair's circle was validity. Their chief question was this: faced with a given argument, what are the rules which will enable me to determine whether the argument is or is not valid? But Agricola's main concern as a logician was persuasion. His chief question was this: given a thesis that I wish to persuade others to accept, how do I set about finding points which will help me to persuade them? Thus, while Mair wanted to find out whether a given conclusion really does follow from the premiss, Agricola wanted to find a suitable set of premisses for the proposition which he hoped to present as a logical conclusion. In all this we see Agricola's acceptance of logic, not as a kind of sovereign art which holds sway in virtue of its usefulness to all the sciences, but instead as an art subordinate to rhetoric, the art of persuasion by well-chosen words.

The second edition of his *Compendium* leaves us in no doubt that William Cranston was deeply influenced by the humanist programme Agricola set out in his *De inventione dialectica*, but it is not clear whether he underwent a grand change of mind after the appearance of the first edition. It may be that even in 1540 Cranston was unhappy about the scholastic conception of logic, and that it then took him several years to make a public declaration of his dissatisfaction. When the public declaration came it was dramatic. He goes so far as to affirm in 1545 that the logician and the orator differ only in respect of the orator's eloquence. Of course, if logic is to be conceived of as primarily a useful instrument for the orator then the thousands of rules the scholastic logicians had painstakingly compiled are mere dead-weight. Nobody is going to persuade people of anything very much by invoking highly artificial rules couched in language nobody understands except scholastic logicians, and if the rules do not persuade anybody then the rules can profitably be ignored. They could not be denied; it was not suggested that they failed to do the job they were devised for. It was simply that the world had moved on, abandoning the rules as the outdated intellectual baggage of an earlier age.

We should remember that logic was a compulsory element of the Arts curriculum, and if the compulsion was to remain then the subject had to be seen to contribute towards fitting the students for the new age. The students (and their parents who, in many cases, were providing financial support) were coming to think that time spent 'logic chopping' was time wasted in that age of rapid economic expansion in which more and more students were aiming to become merchants, secular lawyers, and holders of civic office. William Cranston was attuned to the new mood, and in Scotland no one moved faster than he did to provide the new sort of logic book required in the changed climate.

Patrick Tod was almost as fast. His *Dialecticae methodus* [*Method of Logic*] was published in Paris in 1544. The main body of the work is as terse as the first edition of Cranston's *Compendium*, though without the diagrammatic mode of exposition, but the preface is more expansive, and indicates Tod's humanist sympathies. He congratulates his age, in which liberal disciplines are passed on with the revived study of languages, and very famous authors are brought from the shade to the school, and from darkness to light. The languages referred to in the preface are Greek and classical Latin. The book itself is written in Ciceronian style, and Greek terms and phrases are used on occasion. The book is unoriginal, intentionally so. Tod's method was to gather together points gleaned from 'the prolix and excessively verbose commentaries of others'. In fact Tod hardly needed to turn to the commentaries of others, for there is very little in the book that is not to be found in Aristotle. The process which led to Robert Rollock's logic lectures is already well under way.

William Cranston died in 1562 two years after demitting office as provost of St Salvator's College in St Andrews. He was succeeded in that post by John Rutherford from Jedburgh, a friend of George Buchanan and his brother Patrick, and tutor in the household of Montaigne.[83] Since it would take us too far from strictly philosophical matters it would be inappropriate to dwell upon Rutherford's opposition to certain Scottish reformers, especially to Andrew Melville of whose leanings to the French humanist logician and philosopher Peter Ramus, Rutherford strongly disapproved – though it should be added that Ramus influenced numerous Scots, including John Johnston, Charles Ferme, and the theologian John Cameron. It is probable that Rutherford, as an opponent of Ramus, was in a minority among Scottish scholars.[84]

None of the books so far referred to were published in Scotland. By the 1550s Scottish presses were at last able to cope with the demands of scholars, and Rutherford's sole book

Commentariorum de arte disserendi libri quatuor [*Four books of commentaries on the art of reasoning*] appeared in Edinburgh in 1557. A second edition appeared twenty years later in the year of the author's death. The second edition revealed something further of Rutherford's philosophical stance in so far as he added a preface containing an effusive reference to the anti-Stoic Scottish lawyer Edward Henryson. But apart from that, and friendlier references to Plutarch in the second edition, the two editions are much the same. The book, written in Ciceronian Latin, with a good deal of Greek, is a commentary on Aristotle's logic. Rutherford reveals little or no knowledge of the important advances made in logic in the late-medieval period, concerning for example the effect that a term's position in a proposition has on the sense of the proposition. Nothing was more damaging to the development of logic in the renaissance than the failure to hold on to that advance. It should be said that the late-medieval theory concerning the importance of the order of terms in a proposition developed within the context of their investigation of the theory of supposition. But the theory of supposition was far from characteristic of the logic textbooks of the renaissance. This is not surprising, since Aristotle does not discuss supposition or show any sign that he grasped the concept, and renaissance logicians, determined to return to, and stay with, the original texts of Aristotle, were not likely to investigate areas of logic of which their master knew nothing.

I do not wish to give the impression that Rutherford has nothing new to say whatsoever; there are occasional glimpses of something different. For example, Aristotle, followed by the humanists, discusses the quantifier terms 'every', 'some', and 'none'. Rutherford is certainly taking a step out of the routine when he adds 'few', 'many', 'often' (i.e. 'many times') as signs of particularity along with 'some'. In recent years logicians such as Peter Geach have attended to the question of the role that such terms play in valid inferences (can we, for example, argue that since most As are B, and most Bs are C, most As are C?) However, I think that the main significance of Rutherford's book lies in the fact that it is a particularly fine example of the humanists' attempt to return to the pure thought of Aristotle, to understand him, not through scholastic categories but, instead, as Aristotle's contemporaries might have done.

Amongst Rutherford's contemporaries was John Dempster from Aberdeen. His *Dialogus de argumentatione* was published in Paris in 1554. It is in the literary style of a Platonic dialogue, but in respect of content owes more to Aristotle than to any other author. The subject is valid argument. Dempster starts by noting that an argument cannot be the first act of mind, for an argument is itself a complex act which is only possible because other things have been grasped by the intellect and recorded in the memory. However most of the *Dialogus* is taken up with a discussion of the kind of argument on which Aristotle focused, the 'syllogism', that is, an inference in which a conclusion is drawn from two premisses, where each premiss is a simple proposition, that is to say, of the form 'A is B'. Much of Dempster's discussion does not extend beyond Aristotle. One point where it does do so concerns the syllogistic form known as the 'fourth figure'. The reason for this name need not concern us here. 'Every A is B, and no B is C; therefore no C is A' and 'Some A is B, and every B is C, therefore some C is A' are of the form in question. Aristotle does not discuss syllogisms of this form nor indicate that he recognises their existence. Some medieval commentators refer to it, but reject it as unsatisfactory, the great sixteenth-century philosopher Zabarella doing so on the grounds that it was somehow 'unnatural' to reason by means of fourth figure syllogisms. But Dempster was quite right. There are indeed valid inference forms in the fourth figure, and Dempster lists five of them. In this respect he showed himself more perceptive than many of his contemporaries.

Dempster was, then, prepared on occasion to strike out on his own. William Davidson from Aberdeen was less willing to do this. Unlike his brother John, who became the first Protestant principal of the University of Glasgow, William remained a Catholic and remained active in Catholic circles (he was, for example, a regent at the University of Paris and an associate of the humanist Giovanni Ferrerio there).[85] In his *Institutes* on Aristotle's works on logic he gives a luminously clear account of Aristotle's *Organon* which he had evidently read in Greek, if one may judge by his extensive use of Greek terms.

His book is strongly reminiscent of Rutherford's. He was one of many Scots in the Rutherford mould, in the sense that they were Aristotelian purists concerned to provide a faultless exposition of the master's ideas. Other Scottish scholars who should be mentioned in this connection are Robert Boyd of Trochrig (graduate of Edinburgh University, who became Principal of Glasgow University in 1615), Walter Donaldson, Arthur Johnston, Gilbert Burnet, Andrew Aidie, and Scots associated particularly with Leiden such as John Murdison and Gilbert Jack.[86] Among these men Aristotle was a guru. But this should not be allowed to conceal the fact that Cicero also was a dominant figure. He was commonly called the wisest of men, his literary style was adopted by very many of the philosophers to whom I have referred, and the sample arguments that he used to illustrate logical points expressed in many cases morally worthy sentiments of the kind which he would certainly have endorsed. Instead of being told that Socrates is not a donkey, which is typical of the sample propositions that the scholastics used, the humanist Scots preferred to tell us such things as that probity benefits the state.

A further Scot in the Rutherford mould was Robert Balfour (d. *c.* 1625) from Tarrie in Angus, a pupil of Rutherford. Balfour wrote two Commentaries on Aristotle,[87] quoting numerous Greek sources from Homer to Philo Judaeus and Plotinus and he quotes in addition several humanist heroes such as Rudolph Agricola,

Lorenzo Valla, and Peter Ramus. Balfour's sympathies are thus not in question. His chief aim is to see Aristotle without using the distorting lens provided by the scholastic commentators. This is not to say that he does not go beyond Aristotle at all. For example, he discusses a topic we have already mentioned in connection with Dempster's work, the fourth figure of the syllogism, but Dempster's account is a good deal more reliable.

Balfour does not manage entirely to escape the influence of characteristically medieval doctrines. For example, medieval logicians, unlike Aristotle, dealt with the question of whether it was possible to provide rules which would permit the evaluation of inferences in which not all the propositions were in the present tense. Aristotle ignored this topic since he was concerned with scientific reasoning, and that deals only with universal truths which are expressed in timelessly present-tensed propositions. But the medievals probed the logic of tensed propositions deeply. And some pale reflections of their subtle and complex discussions occur in Balfour's Commentary, as when he observes that 'Every harlot was a virgin; therefore someone who was a virgin is a harlot' is valid. (I should add that medieval logicians considered just such examples – the harlot who was a virgin is a denizen of numerous scholastic logic textbooks – and they would all, so far as I know, have denied that Balfour's sample inference is valid. For let us suppose that every harlot who ever lived was a virgin, and that no harlot now lives. In that case the premiss of Balfour's inference would be true, and the conclusion, since it implies the present existence of a harlot, would be false). However, Balfour was in general successful in one aspect of his humanist aim, for very little medieval logic indeed could be gleaned from the pages of his Commentary.

In his Commentary on the *Nicomachean Ethics* Balfour is again concerned to stay as close as possible to Aristotle's own words. He examines the work in the light of Aristotle's theory of four kinds of cause. These are (1) the final cause, this being the end to which a thing is drawn, much as a lover is drawn to the beloved or an embryo is drawn towards what constitutes the realisation of its full potential; (2) the efficient cause, which precedes its effect and pushes it into a new state, as for example the gardener is the efficient cause of the movement of the wheelbarrow; (3) the formal cause, which is the nature or essence of the thing, as for example the quenching of fire in the clouds is (according to Aristotle) the essence of thunder; (4) the material cause, the matter out of which a thing is formed, as for example wool is the material cause of a scarf. Balfour asserts that for Aristotle the final cause of good acts is happiness; the efficient cause is right reason, or the faculty of will which is governed by right reason – Balfour subsequently clarifies this point by saying that it is the will-governed-by-right-reason, and not right reason as such, which is the efficient cause. The formal cause is virtue, which is a character-disposition to act in accordance with a principle of right reason; and the material cause of good acts is desire or passion. As regards this last cause, it should be stressed that Balfour does not despise passion; it is as much a part of our nature as reason is, and is bad only if reason is not a moderating influence upon it.

Balfour had a deep awareness of the usefulness of the intellectual disciplines. He displays that awareness in his Commentary on Aristotle's logic, for there he declares that logic sheds light upon all the other arts, by giving form to the method of enquiry of all the other arts, and it aids the making of sound connections and the exposing of 'monstrous and false connections'. In the Commentary on Aristotle's *Nicomachean Ethics* Balfour applauds moral philosophy for its usefulness. He declares that no part of philosophy is more fertile or more fruitful than ethics, which supplies us with the concept of living well. Its teaching, which has been placed in us by nature, assists and increases the seeds of the virtues. The Commentary, which is twice the length of the *Nicomachean Ethics*, gives a careful exposition of the text, without advancing many adventurous opinions of its own. Its vigorous and elegant literary style would no doubt, fully in keeping with Balfour's belief in the usefulness of ethics, have the effect of leading his students to a study of Aristotle's own contribution to moral philosophy.

Balfour was not the only renaissance Scot with a particular interest in ethics. Another was Florence Volusenus (or Wilson) from Moray, who studied at Aberdeen University under Mair's colleague Hector Boece, and then at Paris from 1526 where he was a contemporary and friend of George Buchanan. Volusenus was deeply imbued with humanist ideals. He studied the writings of Erasmus, and of Melanchthon who appears to have strongly influenced him; and he knew well the writings of the Italian humanists. He ended his days in the 1550s in Lyons, which at that time had the nearest thing in France to Plato's Academy.

Volusenus's first book, *Commentatio quaedam theologica* (Lyons, 1539), is a devotional work, largely in the style of a litany. Wilson stresses man's dependence upon God: 'O my mind, you are indeed subject to God, your salvation is indeed from Him, He is assuredly your Father who possessed, made, and created you'; we mortals, made from coarse visible matter, do not clearly perceive the invisible God, mighty king of the ages – 'Therefore to You, immortal invisible King, God alone, let all the honour be and all the glory'.[88]

Volusenus occasionally refers to God in humanist terms. For example he speaks of 'the highest Jupiter'[89] and 'ruler of immense Olympus'.[90] Nevertheless Volusenus's God is the Christian God, and knowledge of Him is, affirms Volusenus, man's goal. This is the main message of *De animi tranquillitate dialogus* (Lyons, 1543). A tranquil mind is one steadily at peace with itself and devoid of a tumult of passions. Volusenus asks how such a mind is to be achieved. Its efficient cause is the 'sedation' of the passions,[91] presented as an anti-Stoic doctrine. Volusenus attributes to the Stoics the view that all passions are bad, a view he judges absurd. His own view is that tranquility does not involve an absence of passions, but an absence of a 'tumult' of passions. On this matter Aristotle is judged to have spoken truly in saying that our passions should be subject to the moderating influence of reason[92]; when thus subject they are not evil. Here Volusenus quotes Plutarch: the passions are a part of our nature, and only the impertinent would call nature the author of evil.[93]

But Volusenus, like Balfour, saw ethics as a useful art; and to be useful it would be as well for not all of it to be as abstract as the foregoing remarks about the passions. So he lists numerous practical principles and discusses them in some detail. For example, he writes: 'We should not judge to be our property things which belong to others . . . Shamefully and vainly do we seek rest in external things . . . Vainglory disturbs the peace of human society and impels to every sort of injury . . . Since you are the servant, not the master, of providence, obey willingly and cheerfully.' From the last precept he concludes that we should despise death. He holds it not to be an evil, and points out that the endurance of suffering unto death can be an imitation of Christ. Which of course does not imply that we should set out enthusiastically in search of suffering, 'for suffering is not consistent with the happiness of life now or in the future. For it greatly impedes contemplation and the study of wisdom, in which happiness has been placed'.[94] In all this there is as much theology as philosophy. The theology reveals that Volusenus, though strongly influenced by renaissance humanism, was not in the least a reforming spirit in the religious sense of the term. He was a member of the old order.

The sixteenth century was in many ways a very complicated century for philosophy in Scotland; we could hardly expect otherwise of the century of the Reformation. But to sum it up, it can be argued that there was both loss and gain. There were valuable gains made by the circle of John Mair in the first few decades, and there was a loss since some advances made by those

immensely able men were discarded by the generation of philosophers which followed them. But that loss was itself accompanied
by a gain in so far as there was a return to Aristotle, and in
particular to the original Greek texts, scientifically edited for the
first time. The recovery of those texts was perhaps the single
most important achievement of the humanists, and whether or
not it was a gain sufficient to outweigh the loss just described, it
represented an immense step forward. Scots played their due part
in this process, and helped to secure for the sixteenth century
the right to an honourable mention in works on the history of
philosophy in Scotland.

Of course some of those to whom I have been attending lived
into the seventeenth century, Balfour, for example, dying in
1625. But it is not my purpose in this book to give a continuous
history of Scottish philosophy, and I shall not dwell long on
seventeenth-century developments. I am concerned in this book
to present and defend a certain view concerning the place of
the Enlightenment in Scottish philosophy, and in particular to
argue that even though it is no doubt the highest point reached
in Scottish philosophy, it is by no means the only event of
significance in that history, for the circle of John Mair should
be credited with achievements which are worthy of the closest
attention, and which ensure that any well-balanced account of
the Scottish philosophical tradition must give due space to the
sixteenth century, particularly the first few decades of it.

Philosophy continued to be a major item on the curricula of
the universities. And, as in the preceding century, it remained
open to a wide range of influences from the Continent, including
Spanish Jesuits and Italian humanists.[95] Thus for example in his
inaugural lecture as regent in Arts at Glasgow University Robert
Baillie discusses the role of the active intellect, and his discussion
makes clear the influence upon him of the Paduan philosopher
Zabarella. Concepts central to both metaphysics and theology
are at work in Baillie's lecture, and the concepts are Aristotle's,

though seen through scholastic, or perhaps one should say 'neo-scholastic' eyes. Aristotle writes: 'Since in every class of things, as in nature as a whole, we find two factors involved, (1) a matter which is potentially all the particulars included in the class, (2) a cause which is productive in the sense that it makes them all (the latter stands to the former as e.g. an art to its material), these distinctive elements must likewise be found within the soul' [*De Anima* III 6]. The active part of the soul, termed the 'active intellect' is described by Aristotle as 'separable', that is, it can be 'set free from its conditions' and is 'immortal and eternal'. Zabarella pursued this line of thought to its logical conclusion. Aristotle thought of active intellect as wholly lacking matter; it is, on the contrary, pure form. But there are only two kinds of pure form in Aristotle's system. To one kind belong the pure intellects which are responsible for the motions of the heavenly bodies, and to the other belongs only God. There is no sense in identifying the active intellect with the movers of the heavenly bodies, and therefore the active intellect of human beings must be identified with God. And since God is one it follows that all humans share a single active intellect, which is the ultimate active principle not only of humans but also of the world itself. Baillie's introduction of such themes into his Glasgow teaching shows that scholastic themes, and indeed scholastic modes of thinking were far from dead even decades after the humanist encroachment into the universities of Scotland.

Even clearer evidence of this is found in the thoughts of an unknown Glasgow regent in Arts who makes use of the Jesuit concept of 'middle knowledge' [*scientia media*], which is a concept of the knowledge which God possesses of what a person would have done if he did not do what he did but did something else instead. The thought here has many ramifications. One concerns the fact that the apparently innocent, such as infants, suffer; and their suffering seems incompatible with the infinite goodness of God. Perhaps, therefore, we should say that even if the person had not done evil, or at any rate evil which justified what befell him, then had he lived longer, or been placed in other circumstances, he would have done evil which would have merited his suffering. This requires that God have just as precise knowledge of what would have happened as He is taken to have of what actually happened. This divine knowledge of hypotheticals is called 'middle knowledge' and was the central concept in a bitter theological dispute in which Jesuit theologians were chief protagonists. We learn something of the philosophical and theological climate in Scottish universities in the mid-seventeenth century from the fact that aspects of this debate could be aired in a philosophy lecture to Arts undergraduates.

The same regent who discussed middle knowledge also taught ethics, and was highly critical of the Aristotelian concept of happiness, holding it to be a sham. The Christian concept, which defines happiness in terms of the agent's relation to Christ, was true coinage as compared with the pagan counterfeit of Aristotle's school, which saw happiness as the activity of the soul in accordance with virtue. But some years later James Dalrymple reaffirmed the value of the ethics which were so roundly criticised by that anonymous regent, and even recommended the teaching of the neglected academic discipline of political theory.

Not all the significant Scottish philosophy of the seventeenth century was written in a university context. In the last year of his life James Dundas, first Lord Arniston (*c.*1620–1679), wrote a book *Idea philosophiae moralis* [*The Idea of Moral Philosophy*], that merits close study. He was a relative, through his wife Marion, of two significant Scottish theologians, Robert Boyd of Trochrig, principal of Glasgow University, and Zachary Boyd, vice-chancellor of Glasgow University. Dundas covered a wide range of topics including the nature of good and evil, the concepts of will, of virtue and vice, and he ends (abruptly because death stayed his hand) while writing on moral issues concerning killing, namely suicide, duelling and war. His knowledge of the philosophy of his own era was wide and deep. He invokes, for example, Descartes, Gassendi, Lipsius, Grotius, Henry More and Samuel Rutherford, as well as referring to a number of medieval philosophers and many from the classical period. Two broad characteristics of Dundas's moral philosophy may be mentioned. First, he wrote in a way that reflected his religious stance, giving due consideration, from a specifically theistic standpoint, to philosophical positions, such as those of Epicurus and Hobbes, that he judged to be atheistic. Secondly, Dundas's concept of moral philosophy was practical, for, on his concept of a moral philosopher, not only does such a person have an insight into the nature of virtue and into ways in which unbridled desires can be tamed, and tranquility and happiness achieved, but also these same insights inform the moral philosopher's actions.[96]

As the century wore on the influence of Descartes became increasingly noticeable, though he had his detractors as well as defenders, and the interest in him was at least as much in his scientific speculations as in his philosophy. However he could not be ignored, and it was recognised that a place had to be found for him in the proposed common Arts course of the four Scottish universities. In some ways the most important development in the Scottish philosophical scene in the latter part of the seventeenth century was the attempt to have an agreed Arts curriculum for all the universities.[97] But this move, whatever its pedagogical merits, could not lead to any advance in philosophy itself, and the story of the proposal is of more interest to historians of education than to historians of philosophy. Scotland was, philosophically speaking, biding its time. The lively philosophical spirit, still clearly evident in the country, was awaiting a catalyst. As we all know, it duly came.

8 A Science of Human Nature

Though a line of philosophical influence can be traced from Mair's circle to the philosophers of the Scottish Enlightenment, it is my purpose in this book to seek to identify philosophical relations between the earlier and the later periods rather than historical causal ones. For example, one is occasionally led to wonder whether Thomas Reid, greatest of the members of the eighteenth-century Scottish school of common sense philosophy, had read the Pre-Reformation philosophers given the similarity between certain of his most characteristic doctrines and doctrines of the earlier philosophers, and given also that the writings of those earlier philosophers were in the libraries of the two Scottish universities which he attended. But I shall leave that historical question aside, and focus primarily on philosophical matters, in particular the doctrines shared by the two periods. There are very many studies of the philosophy of the Scottish Enlightenment, and I shall not here be giving a general account of the achievements of that extraordinary event. My concern is very much more with those philosophical relations, already referred to, with Pre-Reformation teaching. In particular I shall be attending to the eighteenth-century versions of medieval nominalism and of the theory of notions, especially to the versions found in the writings of Hume and Reid. For reasons which will become apparent a suitable starting point is a theory by the first great philosopher of the Scottish Enlightenment, Francis Hutcheson.

In 1729 Francis Hutcheson was elected professor of philosophy at the University of Glasgow following the death of Gershom Carmichael, first professor of moral philosophy at

Glasgow, from whose writings he learned a great deal, especially in the fields of ethics and jurisprudence.[98] Hutcheson's name is first associated with the University in 1710/11 when he is listed as a student in the logic class. He entered the university as a fourth year student as he had already covered the material taught in the first three years while still a student at the dissenting academy at Killyleagh, County Down, run by Rev James McAlpine, a Glasgow graduate. After leaving the University, qualified in both Arts and Divinity, he went back to Ireland, first to Ulster (where he gravitated to the side of the non-subscribers in a dispute concerning whether presbyterian ministers should have to subscribe to the Westminster Confession); and then in 1720 to Dublin where he established a presbyterian academy. In 1725 he published *An Inquiry into the Original of our Ideas of Beauty and Virtue*, followed in 1728 by *An Essay on the Nature and Conduct of the Passions and Affections*. These ground-breaking works made his name, and were a main reason for the invitation he received in 1739 to return to Glasgow to take up a philosophy chair. In 1730 his post in Glasgow was more precisely defined; he was to be Professor of Moral Philosophy, and thereafter it was as a moral philosopher that he made his reputation as a teacher, and it is as a moral philosopher that he is now known. One of his pupils, Adam Smith (a successor of Hutcheson's as professor of moral philosophy at Glasgow), referred to him as 'the never to be forgotten Hutcheson', and indeed Smith clearly had many of Hutcheson's ideas in mind when he came to write his own *The Theory of Moral Sentiments*. Another philosopher who had Hutcheson in mind while writing his own masterpiece was Hume. I shall come to that matter later. For the present I shall attend to one of the most influential of Hutcheson's ideas.

Hutcheson considers the term 'sense' as it is used in such phrases as 'the five senses'. Used in this way the term can be defined as follows: 'it is a determination of our minds to receive ideas independently of our will, and to have perceptions of pleasure and pain'.[99] Understanding 'sense' in that way, Hutcheson concludes that we have far more senses than the five that most people would list. First, there are the five senses, referred to by Hutcheson as the 'external senses', sight, hearing, smell, taste, and touch. These clearly involve 'a determination of our mind to receive ideas independently of our will'. Thus for example, I open my eyes and see a sheet of paper. The visual concept I thereupon have of the piece of paper owes nothing to an act of my will. Once my eyes are open and focused upon the paper I have a visual experience of it which it is not within the power of my will either to produce or to prevent. Secondly we have a power of receiving 'pleasant perceptions arising from regular, harmonious, uniform objects', and from 'grandeur and novelty'. This power is the power of 'internal sense'. Thirdly there is a 'publick sense', which is 'our determination to be pleased with the happiness of others, and to be uneasy at their misery'. Fourthly there is the 'moral sense, "by which we perceive virtue or vice in ourselves or in others" '. Fifthly Hutcheson lists a 'sense of honour, "which makes the approbation, or gratitude of others, for any good actions we have done, the necessary occasion of pleasure; and their dislike, condemnation, or resentment of injuries done by us, the occasion of the uneasy sensation called shame" '.

These different kinds of sense are of course directed to objects appropriate to them. Thus the sense of sight is directed to visual properties, and the moral sense is directed to virtue and vice. Hutcheson speaks also about desires which 'arise in our mind, from the frame of our nature', where those desires are of different kinds corresponding to the different kinds of sense through which we grasp the existence of things. These are said to be 'original desires'. One can instance as original desires the desire for virtue, the desire for visual or auditory beauty, and so on. Since we can remember and reason, and are not confined merely to present things, secondary desires arise, desires, that is, for those things which will increase our chance of satisfying original desires. Thus for example desire for wealth is to be classed as secondary. Without the original desires, the secondary desires would not exist. In a telling phrase Hutcheson speaks of the original desires as 'implanted in our nature'.

The third of the kinds of sense listed above, the moral sense, and the corresponding desire for virtue (with its accompanying aversion to vice), lie at the heart of Hutcheson's ethical system. But we should not lose sight of the comparison Hutcheson draws between that sense and the exterior senses. In both cases what is being referred to is something presented with irresistible force to the mind. 'Irresistible' because the will is rendered irrelevant. By the original constitution of our nature we have a visual experience when we open our eyes in daylight just in front of a visible object, and we have an auditory experience when a sound occurs close to our well-functioning ears. These experiences give rise to judgements from which we cannot, by an act of will, withhold our assent concerning the presence of the objects of the experience.

It is crucial for Hutcheson that our knowledge of those objects is immediate, not mediate; we have only to open our eyes to see, and open our ears to hear. There is no question of having to engage in a process of inference whose conclusion would be that we are seeing an object of such and such a kind. Of course, in some cases we can thus reason, as when the object is in some way obscure to our vision, but we know what the obscure object must be, given that it lies in a certain direction or at a certain distance. But we cannot know visible objects with the aid of reason unless there are some visible objects which we know immediately, that is, by simply looking and seeing what is there.

Hutcheson's central doctrine is that the kinds of things just said about the external senses are true also of the moral sense: by the original constitution of our nature we sense the virtuousness of certain acts, and sense the viciousness of others. The recognition of the virtue or vice is irresistible, there being no room for the will to be engaged. We find ourselves responding the way we do to such actions, they please us in a certain way, or displease us, and that we respond in that way is as much a fact of the constitution of our nature as the fact that we see what we see and hear what we hear. It is therefore idle to ask for the role of reason in all our judgements concerning the virtuousness or viciousness of acts. Although it is true that we can reason our way to a judgement in some cases, this is only because there are other cases where our moral sense is immediately active, informing us, without any deliberative act taking place, that such and such an act is virtuous or is vicious. Put otherwise, moral beliefs have a natural non-rational basis. They arise in us by our original constitution, and it is inappropriate to seek to give a rational justification for them; 'inappropriate' since the search for a rational justification implies that the beliefs were reached by a process of reasoning, whereas in fact not all of them can be. There is always a non-rational element, just as there is a non-rational element when we believe something to exist because we can see that it does. What room is there for reason if we can see the object?

Likewise it is Hutcheson's view, basic to his theory of aesthetics, that faced with something sublime or beautiful, an approval wells up in us. The approval is not rational, but must be explained in terms of the original constitution of our nature; we are so made that that is how we do respond. What we see to be beautiful we cannot also prove to be so, and the aesthetic approval is therefore not mediated by rational process. Hutcheson's concept of an original constitution of our nature was taken over by David Hume and worked out in directions of which Hutcheson almost certainly had never dreamed.

It is to Hume that I now turn. He was born in Edinburgh in 1711 and attended Edinburgh University for about four years c.1721–25, studying in all probability Latin, Greek, logic, metaphysics and natural philosophy, this last including discoveries by Robert Boyle and Isaac Newton. Thereafter he worked intensively on the classics and on philosophy, later declaring of that period that: 'there seem'd to be open'd up to me a new Scene of Thought, which transported me beyond Measure . . . '.[100] During the period 1734–7 he was in France, mostly at the village of La Flèche in Anjou, preparing a draft of his philosophical magnum opus *A Treatise of Human Nature*, of which the first two volumes were published (anonymously) in 1739 and the third (also anonymously) in 1740. Hume wrote bluntly about the book's reception: 'Never literary attempt was more unfortunate than my Treatise of Human Nature. It fell *dead-born from the press*, without reaching such distinction, as even to excite a murmur among the zealots.'[101] In fact Hume understated the immediate impact of the *Treatise*; whether or not it started a murmur among the zealots it certainly and immediately began to provide philosophical stimulation for Thomas Reid, greatest of the members of the Scottish school of common sense philosophy. In 1745 Hume's application for the Chair of Moral Philosophy at Edinburgh University was rejected because he was unacceptable to a number of ministers who had a say in the appointment. In 1751 an attempt to secure for him the Chair of Logic and Rhetoric at Glasgow failed for the same reason. By the latter date he had published two sets of *Essays, Moral and Political*, (1741 and 1742) and the *Philosophical Essays Concerning Human Understanding* (1748) (a revised edition of which was published in 1756 under the title *An Enquiry Concerning Human Understanding*). In 1751 he also published *An Enquiry Concerning the Principles of Morals*, 'which', he affirmed, 'in my own opinion (who ought not to judge on that subject), is of all my writings, historical, philosophical or literary, incomparably the best'.[102] In that same year Hume, by then a distinguished man of letters, became librarian of the Library of the Faculty of Advocates in Edinburgh. During the following eleven years he published a six-volume *History of England* (1754–62) and *Four Dissertations* (1757). Thereafter his principal employment was a series of posts, including chargé d'affaires at the British Embassy in Paris. Hume died in 1776. Adam Smith, Hume's closest friend and the person philosophically closest to him in Scotland, spoke from the heart: 'Upon the whole, I have always considered him, both in his lifetime, and since his death, as approaching as nearly to the idea of a perfectly wise and virtuous man, as perhaps the nature of human frailty will admit.'[103] There were, however, zealots in the land, who judged Hume to be neither wise nor virtuous, and, worst of all, not even a believer. Three years after his death Hume spoke again, as if from the grave. His *Dialogues Concerning Natural Religion*, possibly the greatest work on natural theology to have come out of the Enlightenment, was published. No doubt zealots reading the book would be confirmed in their judgement that Hume was an atheist. But whether he was an atheist or not is in fact not a question easily settled on the basis of the *Dialogues*, and the issue remains contested.

In the first sentence of Part I of *A Treatise of Human Nature* Hume writes: 'All the perceptions of the human mind resolve themselves into two distinct kinds, which I shall call IMPRESSIONS and IDEAS.' This distinction, which is of the first importance for both the content and the mode of exposition of his philosophy, soon established itself as a major battleground, a fact which must have greatly disappointed Hume's expectations, for he affirms: 'I believe it will not be very necessary to employ many words in explaining this distinction. Every one of himself will readily perceive the difference betwixt feeling and thinking'.[104] Clearly Hume was making a distinction that he thought would be readily understood and accepted, and we should therefore seek as far as we can to interpret his account of the distinction in such a way that we could easily imagine him supposing it to be readily understandable and acceptable.

Hume did not do himself any favours in the way he expounded it. We see an object and then think about it, hear a sound and then think about it, undergo an emotion and then think about it. In each case something is present on a first occasion, and then it is present again, but only in our minds, where it is 're-presented'. Hume focuses on two differences between the presentation and the re-presentation. One is the fact that the presentation has greater 'force', 'violence', 'liveliness' or 'vivacity' (all of which appear to mean the same thing, as Hume uses them in this context), and the re-presentation has less. The other is that, as is obvious, the presentation precedes the re-presentation. The presentation is termed an 'impression', and the re-presentation, which he calls a 'faint image', is termed an 'idea'. Thus Hume writes: 'Those perceptions, which enter with most force and violence, we may name *impressions*; and under this name I comprehend all our sensations, passions and emotions, as they make their first appearance in the soul. By *ideas* I mean the faint images of these in thinking and reasoning'.[105]

Evidently Hume is uneasy about the distinction in so far as it is drawn in terms of degree of liveliness of the perception. He admits, for example, that in sleep, in a fever, or in madness, or in any violent emotional state, our ideas may approach the degree of liveliness of impressions; and he admits also that sometimes our impressions are so faint and low that we cannot distinguish them from ideas. For the most part, then, impressions are livelier than ideas. This means that degree of liveliness is an inadequate criterion for determining whether a given perception is or is not an impression.

The criterion of precedence seems better in that respect; an impression always occurs before the corresponding idea. But the matter is not plainsailing. First it is necessary to distinguish between simple and complex ideas. A complex idea may correspond to no impression. Thus by an act of imagination I can form a unitary image out of a variety of several ideas where the complex image corresponds to no impression which I had previously had. And to this Hume replies that a complex idea is formed out of simple ones, and the simple ones are re-presentations of preceding impressions.[106] Had he left the matter there we might have concluded that Hume was, whether right or wrong, at least consistent. However, his claim that we can imagine a shade of a given colour though we had never before had an impression of it undermines his criterion for determining whether a given perception is an impression or an idea. His example is of the missing shade of blue in an otherwise complete presentation of the blue part of the spectrum. Hume affirms: 'this instance is so singular, that it is scarcely worth our observing, and does not merit that for it alone we should alter our general maxim'.[107]

Hume is, however, wrong about its 'singularity', and if what makes his instance 'scarcely worth our observing' is its singularity, then that instance is indeed worth our observing, since it points to a serious flaw in his account of the relations between impressions and ideas. The reason Hume's instance is not singular, is this: if a person can indeed have an idea of a shade of blue, though he had not had a previous impression of that shade, then we have to allow that a person could also have an idea of other missing shades of blue, and also of missing shades of every other colour; and there is no reason why we should restrict ourselves here to a consideration of only the visual one of the five sensory modalities. We could also have an idea of a missing sound, or taste, or smell, or tactile quality. This is not to say that Hume is wrong to insist that there is an order of appearance of impressions and ideas but his formulation is inadequate. Hume might allow that a person can have an idea of a missing shade of blue if he has already had an impression of many shades of blue, but deny that a person could have an idea of blue if he had not previously had an impression of any shade of blue; and all the more might he deny that a person who had never had an impression of a colour could have an idea of one. That is to say, Hume might be on much stronger ground if he holds that we cannot form ideas of a sensory modality wholly new to us.

For all the difficulties in the formulation of the distinction Hume is concerned with, we have to remind ourselves of the fact that he is dealing with something he thinks very familiar to all of us. As he affirms: 'Every one of himself will readily perceive the difference between feeling and thinking.' He expands on that point elsewhere: 'Every one will readily allow, that there is a considerable difference between the perceptions of the mind, when a man feels the pain of excessive heat, or the pleasure of moderate warmth, and when he afterwards recalls to his memory this sensation, or anticipates it by his imagination . . . The most lively thought is still inferior to the dullest sensation.' [108] It is perhaps the very familiarity of the distinction that prevents Hume attending sufficiently to the question of the precise criteria for determining when we are dealing with an impression and when with an idea.

There is ample evidence that Hume's distinction is almost the same as the medieval distinction, so important to John Mair and his colleagues, between intuition and abstraction. The earlier philosophers speak of intensity of a notion where Hume speaks of the liveliness of a perception, and they hold that intuitive and abstractive notions are different in kind and not merely in quality, and hence an abstractive notion can never become intuitive merely by a process of intensification – even, they add, if it becomes infinitely intense. Furthermore they hold that intuitive notions precede the corresponding abstractive ones, while allowing that by an act of imagination a notion can be formed to which no single intuitive notion corresponds. There are however differences between medieval notions and Humean perceptions, and I shall be attending to them later.

Hume noticed that ideas do not occur randomly, but seem

instead to present themselves to us in a more or less orderly or structured way, and he therefore sought the principles of association of ideas. He discovered three. Given an idea of an object X the next idea which occurs, an idea of a Y, is likely to be related to the first in that either (1) object Y resembles object X, or (2) Y is contiguous with X, or (3) Y is a cause or an effect of X. This tendency for ideas to present themselves in an orderly way is described by Hume as 'a gentle force which commonly prevails'; and he speaks of it also as 'a kind of ATTRACTION, which in the mental world will be found to have as extraordinary effects as in the natural, and to shew itself in as many and as various forms'.[109] According to this doctrine ideas attract each other much as, on Newton's theory, particles of matter attract each other. Of course Hume does not provide a mathematical formula of attraction of ideas corresponding to Newton's inverse square law, but there is no doubting the Newtonianism of this part of the *Treatise*, or of the later part where Hume introduces the concept of a principle of association of impressions.

Why is the distinction between impressions and ideas so important? Hume argues that many ideas which philosophers claim to have are not ideas to which there is a corresponding preceding impression, hence nothing exists corresponding to the idea. What is the relation between impression and 'existence'? I think it is this: if I have an impression of an X then I know that the X now exists, whereas if I have an idea of an X I am not, merely in virtue of having the idea, in a position to know whether or not X now exists. I can conjecture, or opine, that it does, but I cannot truly claim knowledge. In medieval terms what is being said (roughly) is that an intuitive notion of X produces evident assent to the proposition affirming the present existence of X. Among the ideas which Hume has in his sights are those of (1) a necessary connection between causally related events, (2) an external world, and (3) a self. If I have not had an impression of a necessary connection, and therefore have not been in a position to claim knowledge of the existence of a necessary connection, then neither can I have an idea of it. If I have not had an impression of an external world and therefore have not been in a position to claim knowledge of such a world, then neither can I have an idea of it. Likewise with my impression of my self.

In Book I of the *Treatise* Hume examines our beliefs in the existence of (1) a necessary connection between a cause and its effect, (2) an external world, and (3) the self. In each case he concludes that there is no rational basis for the belief, that is, he concludes that we have no impressions corresponding to the ideas. He therefore undertakes to provide an account of how we come by the ideas if there are no corresponding impressions. This he does, in some of the most dazzling pieces of philosophy of the Enlightenment. What occurs in this part of Hume's philosophy is central to that philosophy, and I should like to spell out certain aspects of it.

To state the matter simply, Hume (1) notes the three beliefs just listed, (2) notes that to have such beliefs implies that we have an idea of causal necessary connection, of an external world and of a self, (3) notes his doctrine that to our ideas there are antecedent resembling impressions, notes (4) that in fact we have no impressions which correspond in the appropriate way to these three ideas, and concludes (5) that we do not have the ideas in question, even if we (who should surely know best!) think we do. Now, there is a strange aspect to this procedure for determining whether we do or do not have the ideas in question, namely, that we cannot determine whether or not we have the impressions corresponding to the ideas unless we can compare our impressions with the three ideas. How, for example, can I know whether a given impression is an impression of necessary connection if I have no idea of necessary connection? Hence even to begin the search for the impression implies that I have the idea, and yet according to Hume's philosophy it seems that in the absence of a corresponding impression there is no idea either. Thus I use the idea in order to show that I cannot have it. This is absurd. If it is what Hume is saying then this part of his system, and perhaps other parts also, cannot be taken seriously.

But it is not what he is saying. Here we should acknowledge the large role played in Hume's system by the faculty of imagination. Hume, as already noted, allows that we can have complex ideas to which there correspond no preceding unitary impressions. Given some impressions I have already had of various colours and shapes, I can imagine a picture that is based on those earlier impressions but does not correspond to any single preceding impression. Hume is clear on this matter. He holds that the imagination is also at work in the process which results in our possession of the ideas of necessary connection and so on. He holds that we do indeed have an idea of necessary connection but that that idea is a product of imagination and does not correspond to a preceding unitary impression, just as, to take an example of Hume's, I can have an idea of the New Jerusalem even though I have never had an impression of it. I will not get an idea of necessary connection by observing a single occurrence of a given type of event, say, a single occurrence of a firework throwing off sparks when a match is put to the touchpaper. But when I have seen this happen often I acquire, by purely natural means, a habit of forming a lively idea of the second event in the sequence, an idea of the effect, when I have an impression of the first event, the cause. There is thus a determination of the mind to expect, say, a firework to throw off sparks when a match is put to the touch paper. The determination of the mind is then read by us as a feature in the world, in particular, a feature of the relation between the lighted match and the sparking firework, and that feature is what we call a necessary connection between the lighted match and the sparking firework. It is not in reality such a feature; what we think is external to us is in fact internal, a determination of the mind, and is projected out into the world, where it is held in place by an act of imagination.

Likewise when Hume discusses the fact that we have no impression of an external world, he gives an account of why we come to think that we do, an account that focuses on the role played by our imagination in the construction of a world which we then take to be independent of us when in reality it is in large measure a product of our own imagination. To take the third case, Hume invokes the activity of imagination in explaining how we come by the idea of a self. In Books II and III of the *Treatise*, everything Hume says implies that there is indeed an external world, that the parts of that world are bound together by causal necessity, and that selves inhabit it, and are at home in it. There can be no surprise in the fact that I am at home in the world, for, if Hume is right, it is in large measure a construction of my own imagination.

Yet people do believe in the three things, which Hume has shown to be mainly a product of acts of the imagination. Hume himself continues to believe in the existence of those things – as how could he not, given that they play such an immense role in our experience. He recognises that his practical dealings with the world, including his dealings with his fellow humans, are wholly unaffected by his philosophical destruction of the claim that there is any rational basis to the most important of our beliefs about the world we inhabit. This fact merits attention. It will draw us to an understanding of his relationship to Hutcheson, and will also affect our interpretation of how Hume stands in relation to the school of common sense philosophy.

Hutcheson held that it is by a sense, akin to the sense of sight, that we believe that given acts are virtuous and others vicious, and that given objects are beautiful and others ugly. We are dealing here with an aspect or element of what Hutcheson describes as 'the original frame of our nature'. Asked why we believe a given act to be virtuous we can only reply that we can see it to be so. Faced with the act, approval wells up, or arises, in us; there is not a rational basis to our belief or our approval. A belief's being irresistible carries no implication as to whether there is a rational justification for it, and Hutcheson holds that we have many beliefs concerning ethics and aesthetics which, though irresistible, lack a foundation in reason.

According to an influential interpretation,[110] Hume recognised that Hutcheson's doctrine could be generalised, and then applied to our beliefs about non-moral and non-aesthetic features and constituents of the world, in particular, our beliefs about the necessary connection between a cause and its effect, about the externality of the world, and lastly about the existence of our self. We believe there to be an external world, and our failure to prove that there is one cannot undermine or in the least weaken the belief. That is, the belief is held with such firmness that it could not be held more firmly even if we had succeeded in proving it to be true.

We should remember that the full title of Hume's masterpiece is *A Treatise of Human Nature: Being an Attempt to Introduce the Experimental Method of Reasoning into Moral Subjects*. The term 'moral' is used in a wider sense by Hume than we should think appropriate today. For Hume 'moral subjects' include the whole range of topics concerned with the life of the spirit. The content of our perceptual or aesthetic consciousness is no less a moral subject than is the content of our moral consciousness, and when Hume speaks of 'experimental reasoning' he does not have in mind reasoning based upon experiments. Nowadays we would contrast his 'experimental reasoning' with 'a priori reasoning'. That is, Hume is seeking to draw a map of human nature, not on the basis of an analysis of concepts, or by working from a certain theological position regarding God's nature and purpose. Instead Hume's basis is experience. He hopes to avoid coming, already loaded with a theory, to the question of the identification of the basic features of human nature. His intention instead is to observe human beings and then draw conclusions from his untheoretical observations.

What he observes is people living in accordance with a number of beliefs which they find absolutely irresistible and which have no rational basis. It is not that many or even most people have these beliefs. Everyone has them, Hume included.[111] We are dealing here with something basic to human beings, a set of beliefs which, in Hutcheson's phrase, are 'implanted in our nature'. We have already noted that in discussing 'sense' Hutcheson describes it as a 'determination of our mind to receive ideas independently of our will'. It is just such a determination of our mind by which we have the beliefs we do about causality, externality, and the self. We do not will to believe in the external world, we just do believe in it, and knowing, as Hume did, that there is no rational basis for that belief, but only an imaginative basis, we still cannot will not to believe in it. Or, put otherwise, we can will as hard as we like; it can make no difference. We believe it because it is our nature to do so. Now, Hume has often been characterised as a sceptical philosopher, and the description is in a sense correct, though I think not in the way that it is commonly taken. Hume is indeed sceptical about our basic beliefs, in particular those already enumerated, but his scepticism is directed to the alleged rational basis for them. He is not saying that the beliefs are false, but only that they lack rational justification. Hume does not deny the existence of what we call the external world; what he adds is that that world is largely the outcome of an act of imagination. He does not deny the existence of what we call a necessary connection between cause and effect – on the contrary he tells us in some detail about its constituents and its metaphysical status; what he adds is that that necessary connection is largely the result of the imagination's activity.

There are additional levels of complexity here, and I should like to end this chapter by making a brief comment about one of them. In Book I of the *Treatise* Hume denies that he has an impression of the self, but makes extensive use of the self in Books II and III in the development of his theory of the emotions and in his moral theory. For the latter theories are based on his account of sympathy, which he takes to be a mechanism for the transference of an impression from one person to another, and the theory of emotions is explicitly dependent on the concept of a self, for Hume speaks of the self as the object of the emotions of pride and humility.

In a famous sentence Hume declaims: 'Be a philosopher; but, amidst all your philosophy, be still a man.'[112] The philosopher seeks to determine what can be sanctioned by reason, and seeks also to determine what cannot be thus sanctioned. The fact that some irresistible beliefs cannot be sanctioned by reason does not imply that it is inappropriate for them to be accorded a place in a philosophical system for in so far as the system contains a systematic study of human nature those beliefs have to be slotted into the overall account of human nature. In addition, in so far as that system includes a system of ethics and therefore discusses the nature of moral judgement, virtue, and justice, it is essential that it include a proper account of human nature. Morality is for human beings, and it would be incredible if a fitting system of morality for human beings was in no way shaped by human nature. Hence the fact that a belief in the self is not sanctioned by reason is irrelevant to the question of whether it is appropriate to make use of the concept in considering human emotions and morality. In order to be justified in making use of the concept it is sufficient that everyone, and irresistibly, believes in the existence of themselves and others.

We cannot however simply ignore the fact that in Book I of the *Treatise* Hume sought an impression of his self (or 'himself') and could not find it: 'when I enter most intimately into what I call *myself*, I always stumble on some particular perception or other, of heat or cold, light or shade, love or hatred, pain or pleasure. I never can catch *myself* at any time without a perception, and never can observe any thing but the perception.'[113] Hume concludes that the self is in reality nothing but a 'bundle or collection of different perceptions', and it is by an act of the imagination that we confer an identity, termed the 'self', upon the bundle. Hume argues that it is by the activity of imagination that we see the bundle of disparate perceptions as possessing an identity – a 'personal identity'. He argues that the sort of act of imagination required for creating an identical self is the same as the sort by which the identity of an object in the external world is created. Thus he concludes that we do after all have an idea of the self, but it is not an idea for which there is a corresponding unitary impression.

He did however think that some philosophers believed our idea of self to be derived from such an impression. The kind of self which Hume sought in vain in Book I was not the kind whose existence he assumed for the remainder of the *Treatise*. In Book I he sought a Cartesian self, a thinking substance for which to exist is to think, and he found no impression of it. But he did find what we call a self, namely a bundle of perceptions. It is this self, a product of imagination, which is the subject of the remainder of the *Treatise*. It turns out to be a social self, a self which develops in society and comes to know itself through its relations with others. This latter kind of self is something of whose existence no person can have any doubt, and Hume acknowledges this in the use he makes of the concept of a self. The precise way to characterise the connection between the Cartesian self and the Humean social self is an interesting and important question, though this is not an appropriate place to pursue it. My aim has been the more limited one of explaining how Hume can, without contradiction, both deny and also affirm the existence of the self.

9   The Common Sense Reaction

Thomas Reid was born in Strachan, Kincardineshire, in 1710, to Lewis Reid, the parish minister, and Margaret Gregory, a member of the Gregory family, the most distinguished academic family of eighteenth-century Scotland, distinguished for its scientists and mathematicians; Margaret Gregory's three brothers were mathematics professors as also was one of her uncles, and several of her Gregory relations were professors of medicine.[114] These details about Reid's family are important for an understanding of Reid the man; for he followed his father into the Kirk ministry, was also, in the tradition of the Gregories, a noted scientist and innovative mathematician, and demonstrated pride in his Gregory connections.

From 1723 to 1726 he was a student at Marischal College, Aberdeen, where he studied under the regent George Turnbull, who took his cohort of students through the whole cycle of arts and science subjects. Turnbull was an early figure in the Scottish school of common sense philosophy, and was arguably a major influence on Reid's philosophical development. In 1733 Reid was appointed Marischal College librarian, an appointment which he probably owed to his connection with the Gregories. He was called to be minister at New Machar, Aberdeenshire, in 1737 and then, in 1751, was appointed regent at King's College, Aberdeen, where he was also a member of the Philosophical Society, the 'Wise Club', whose membership included George Campbell, Alexander Gerard, James Beattie and James Dunbar, and where, more than anywhere, the Scottish common sense philosophy was developed. The Wise Club was the venue for papers by Reid that formed the substance of parts of his *Inquiry into the Human Mind on the Principles of Common Sense*, just as papers read by George Campbell formed the substance of parts of his *Philosophy of Rhetoric* and of his *Dissertation on Miracles*. In 1764 Reid published his *Inquiry into the Human Mind* and in the same year was elected to the chair of Moral Philosophy at Glasgow University in succession to Adam Smith. He occupied the chair till his death in 1796, though in 1780 he gave up his teaching duties, perhaps because he was beginning to lose his hearing, and perhaps also because he wished to prepare his lectures for publication. Till around 1784 he conceived of the proposed publication as a unitary work, but very late in the process of preparation he divided them into two parts, with the *Essays on the Intellectual Powers of Man* appearing in 1785, to be followed three years later by the *Essays on the Active Powers of the Human Mind*. The two sets of *Essays* along with the *Inquiry into the Human Mind* are the most significant documents of the Scottish school of common sense philosophy. Their content is in part negative and in part positive in that the works contain a powerful attack upon Hume's system, and a vigorous defence of an alternative philosophical system, that of common sense.

Reid went to great lengths to make clear the relation between his own philosophical position and Hume's, but it is not as easy as one might suppose to say precisely what that relation is. In this chapter I shall seek to clarify it. We shall see that members of Mair's circle are in ghostly attendance; for a characteristic doctrine of that circle reaches out across a gap of two and a half centuries and takes its place as the central thesis of Reid's philosophy.

Reid's philosophy is in the modern style in respect of its attention to the details of language. A routine move of Reid's is to link his philosophical claims with grammatical ones, and seek support for his philosophy in linguistic practice. Immanual Kant argued that our experience of the world has a structure provided by our faculty of reason, that structure constituting the universal and necessary element in our experience and rendering the world intelligible to us. The structure is articulated in a set of twelve concepts, the twelve categories of the understanding, such as the category of causality, by which we interpret events in terms of a causally necessary connection between one event and its immediate successor.[115] In this century Gottlob Frege gave a large twist to Kant's theory of the categories; he agreed that there are fundamental categories through which we interpret the world, but he held that the categories are linguistic.[116] He had in mind such categories as that of a name and of a predicate. This view lies at the heart of one kind of linguistic philosophy; such a philosophy cannot speak about the fundamentals of human experience without reference to language, and for any of its basic positions support must be found in language.

Reid's philosophy is in a sense a linguistic philosophy, but it is appropriate here to point out one difference between Reid's use of linguistic facts and Frege's. In Frege's view our basic linguistic categories structure our experience of the world; in Reid's view they reflect it: 'I believe no instance will be found of a distinction made in all languages, which has not a just foundation in nature.'[117] Because we have the experiences we do, our language has the features it has. Reid has in mind nouns and verbs, the active voice and passive voice of verbs, the relation between subject and predicate, and so on – we shall shortly see how this works. Since our basic linguistic categories are not accidental but are, so to say, forced upon us by the nature of our experience, it follows that we could practically read our philosophy out of our language. And even if, in our philosophising, we do not start with the linguistic facts, but instead begin with the contents of our experience, perceptual and otherwise, nevertheless we can then turn to the facts of language in search of support for our philosophy. On this view of language it could clearly be a powerful tool in the hands of a philosopher, and no philosopher used it to greater effect than Reid. At every point in his attack on Hume he brings linguistic practice into play by arguing that what Hume claims to be the case is not reflected in language, whereas Reid's own position invariably is, and therefore Reid's position has a greater claim on our support than does Hume's.

It is not however Reid's practice to start by a consideration of the linguistic evidence. Indeed there has to be an articulated position in place before it makes sense to ask for evidence. In his discussion of the nature of definition Reid points out that it is impossible that everything be definable, for definitions are clarification of a certain kind, and some terms are so clear that it is impossible for them to be made clearer. Those clearest of all terms are the terms used in the definitions of other, less clear, terms. What is true of definitions is true also of proofs. In the case of many, or most, propositions it is appropriate to ask for a proof of them. But it is not reasonable to suppose that everything admits of proof. A proof is a demonstration of a proposition on the basis of others, which are the premisses. Perhaps the premisses also can be proved, and so on. But Reid holds that this process must come to a stop. Possession of mediate knowledge, that is, knowledge mediated by premisses, presupposes the existence of immediate knowledge, knowledge which is intuitive rather than discursive. Reid lists a number of principles 'common to philosophers and to the vulgar' which need no proof and do not admit of direct proof, which are the foundation of all reasoning and all science: 'Men need not to be taught them; for they are such as all men of common understanding know; or such, at least, as they give a ready assent to, as soon as they are proposed and understood'.[118] I shall give some of Reid's principles here to indicate the basis of his attack upon Hume.

Reid writes: 'I shall take it for granted, that I *think*, that I *remember*, that I *reason*, and, in general, that I really perform all those operations of mind of which I am conscious'.[119] But he does not simply take it for granted. He has evidence for the existence of these operations, the evidence being that he is conscious of them. I have said that for Reid it does not make sense to ask for a definition for everything, for some things are indefinable. Among the things Reid takes to be such is consciousness. All the same, he comes close to providing a definition when he says that consciousness is an operation of the understanding whose objects are 'all the passions, and all the actions and operations of our own minds, while they are present'.[120] We remember them if they are past, but are conscious of them if they are present. On this account consciousness does not provide immediate evidence of the existence of external objects, desks and trees, and so on, though we can be conscious of looking at or seeing a tree. The immediate object is in the mind. Reid is not following ordinary usage on this matter, since there is no linguistic impropriety in speaking of 'being conscious of music in the background'. I think he is to a degree setting up the term 'consciousness' as a technical term in his philosophy, but using the term to a large extent in a manner concordant with ordinary usage.

He is interested in the concept of consciousness since it plays a role in his first principle of common sense. He writes: 'Every man finds himself under a necessity of believing what consciousness testifies, and every thing that hath this testimony is to be taken as a first principle'.[121] Elsewhere he adds an important clause: 'The existence therefore of those passions and operations of our minds, of which we are conscious, is a first principle, which Nature requires us to believe upon her authority'.[122] For example, if I am conscious of doubting a given proposition, then nature requires me to believe upon her authority that the doubting exists. I cannot doubt and also doubt that I doubt. For Reid the case is the same as with our consciousness of pain. If I am conscious of a pain then the pain really exists, and does so indubitably. Likewise with the other passions and operations of the mind.

The irresistibility of our assent to a judgement of the real existence of the objects of our consciousness leads Reid to the conclusion that we are dealing here with what he terms 'an original power of the mind'. The original power is our power to produce what the medieval philosophers termed 'evident assent' to a judgement of real existence. There is no rational basis to the assent, we have an immediate grasp of its existence, the grasp being an act of consciousness. It is, I think, plain that in his search for first principles of common sense Reid is seeking, like Hume, to draw a map of human nature, and his method is not a priori, but based firmly on the deliverances of experience. Indeed 'an attempt to introduce the experimental method of reasoning into moral subjects', the subtitle of Hume's *Treatise*, could apply equally to Reid's two sets of *Essays*. To be clearer about the relation between Hume and Reid it is necessary to spend more time with the map which Reid draws.

Reid is alive to the problems of attending to the passions and operations of our mind. When we are angry at an insult our attention is directed to the insult and the insulter. That is, it is directed outward; or perhaps we should say that our attention and anger are directed outward. If we then seek to attend to the anger prompted by the insult, we are thereby distracted from the insult; and since it is the insult that caused, and contemplation of the insult that sustains, the anger, the attention which is paid to the anger and not to its object results in the weakening or disappearance of the anger. We can however learn to give attention even to these outward-directed passions and mental operations, though perhaps it is often only by an oblique glance that they can be observed.

The act or operation by which we attend to them is reflection, which Reid describes as a kind of 'intuition' which gives 'a like conviction with regard to internal objects, or things in the mind, as the faculty of seeing gives with regard to objects of sight'.[123] The conviction to which reflection gives rise is not a learned response, but is there by nature. The fact that reflection gives rise to that conviction is an original feature of human nature; we can take note of the existence of the feature, but it is pointless to ask why things are like that. Reid's answer could only be that things just are like that. I think that if pressed further on the matter, Reid would refer, as he often does, to the wise judgement of God whose creatures we are.

All the mental operations of which I am conscious, the thinkings, doubtings, imaginings, remembering, and so on, are operations of *my* mind. I cannot be conscious of them, thinks Reid, without also being conscious of myself as subject of these operations. It is not simply that each of my mental operations has a self as its subject, but rather that there is a single self which is the subject of all of them. Reid writes: 'Every man has an immediate and irresistible conviction, not only of his present existence, but of his continued existence and identity, as far back as he can remember. If any man should think fit to demand a proof that the thoughts he is successively conscious of belong to one and the same thinking principle. If he should demand a proof that he is the same person to-day as he was yesterday, or a year ago, I know no proof that can be given him.'[124] We are faced here, again, with an original feature of human nature, the consciousness each has of himself through his consciousness of his mental acts. For me, that I exist is, in Reid's technical sense, common sense; it neither needs proof nor admits of direct proof, and I cannot resist giving assent to the proposition.

As well as a subject of my mental operations there is also, in most cases, an object which is distinct from the operation itself. The operation of seeing is directed to an object. I cannot see without seeing something. It is not that the act of seeing is somehow incomplete if there is no object to which the act is directed; it is that there is no act of seeing at all. It is important to recognise that the relation between a mental act and its object is not that of whole to part. I cannot remember without remembering something, and what I remember, the object of the act, must be different from the act itself, for the act is present and the object is past. This insight by Reid is accompanied by a reference to its linguistic correlate. I quote the passage as an example of Reid's method: 'The operations of our minds are denoted, in all languages, by active transitive verbs, which, from their construction in grammar, require not only a person or agent, but likewise an object of the operation. Thus the verb know, denotes an operation of mind. From the general structure of language, this verb requires a person; I know, you know, or he knows: But it requires no less a noun in the accusative case, denoting the thing known; for he that knows, must know something . . . '[125]

We are now very close to the heart of Reid's criticism of Hume. Let us start by noting that the term 'idea' has been a favourite term of philosophers at least since the time of Plato, though over the centuries it has changed its sense. During the century from Descartes to Hume a distinctive theory, the 'theory of ideas', was forged which became the dominant philosophical theory on the Continent and in Britain. Hume drew a number of conclusions from the theory. It was Reid's contention that those conclusions were validly drawn. It was also his contention that they were absurd. Reid's own conclusion was that the theory of ideas itself must be absurd, and in a sense the claim that it is absurd is the central negative thesis of the *Essays on the Intellectual Powers*.

Reid's contention might be put simply as follows: ideas, as certain philosophers (notably, Descartes, Locke, Berkeley, and Hume) use the term, do not exist. He accepts of course that, in the ordinary sense of 'idea', we can have ideas. But he holds that ideas, as certain of his philosophical predecessors and contemporaries have used the term, are not in the least like ideas in the ordinary sense. As it is ordinarily understood, and here we go straight to Reid's central thesis and to the heart of his criticism of Hume, an idea is an act or operation of mind. I have an idea of a given object if I think about the object, or perceive, remember, conceive, or imagine it. Thus I can have an idea about what is present to my senses, and about what is absent from them, about what does exist, and about what does not, about what can exist whether it does or not, and about what cannot. In this sense of 'idea', ideas exist, for there are such acts as thinking, conceiving, remembering, and imagining, and ideas are acts such as these. In Reid's own words: 'To think of a thing, and to have a thought of it . . . to conceive a thing, and to have a conception, notion, or idea of it, are phrases perfectly synonymous. In these phrases, the thought means nothing but the act of thinking . . . and the conception, notion or idea, the act of conceiving.'[126] So much, then, for what Reid thought of as the 'ordinary' sense of the term 'idea'. I should like now to turn to his account of the sense of 'idea' as that term is used by Hume and other adherents of the theory of ideas.

When we recall an event X, X is an object of that mental operation. But is there not a problem about how we can make cognitive contact with what no longer exists? Surely it is too late. Yet there is something that we are thinking about when we remember event X. It is true at least that we have a present idea of the event. So why not say that even though we cannot be in direct cognitive contact with the past event, there is no problem attached to the supposition that we can be in direct contact with the present idea of the past event? This allows us to explain how we can be in contact with the past event X for we are in direct contact with our present idea of X, and through that present idea we are in indirect contact with what the idea is an idea of, namely X itself. On this view, then, the direct object of thought, that is, of the recollection, is a present idea. The present idea enables us to overcome the temporal distance between ourselves now and a past event we had experienced, for through that idea we somehow manage to reach back over that distance to the recollected event.

Likewise we can invoke our immediate contact with our own

ideas in order to explain how we can overcome other sorts of distance and make cognitive contact with objects which are imagined, conceived, or seen, and so on. Thus, for example, although a given object is many miles distant from us, we can see it. How do we overcome that distance and make cognitive contact with the object? The short answer is that we do so through our idea of the object. For however distant may be the object, we do not need to overcome any distance at all to make contact with our own idea – we are directly conscious of it.

We are, therefore, concerned here with a theory of cognitive contiguity according to which the mind can act directly only upon objects which are immediately present to it, and those objects are our ideas. This is not to say that we know nothing but our own ideas. But if there is anything that we know that is not our idea, then that thing is known indirectly, for it can be known only through an idea.

This, then, is Reid's interpretation of the theory of ideas. Some might accuse him of setting up a man of straw. I do not want to raise here the question of the merits of such an accusation. For present purposes it is sufficient to have a grasp of his interpretation of the theory which is the chief target of the critical aspect of his *Essays on the Intellectual Powers*. It should therefore be noted that Reid attaches particular importance to certain of Locke's assertions to which I have made reference in an earlier chapter, namely the assertions that the term 'idea' stands for whatever is the object of understanding when a man thinks, or whatever it is that the mind can be employed about in thinking; that the mind perceives nothing but its own ideas; and that all knowledge consists in the perception of the agreement of our ideas.

Locke does not seek to argue that we can have no knowledge of what is external to the mind; on the contrary he argues that we do have such knowledge. His point however is that that knowledge is indirect, for it is mediated by our knowledge of those of our ideas which are caused in our mind by external objects. On Reid's interpretation of this point, Locke is claiming not only that ideas should be treated as evidence for the existence of the external objects which are the causes of those ideas, but furthermore that certain qualities of the ideas permit us to draw conclusions about the qualities of the external causes of the ideas. Thus ideas stand in two distinct relations to their external causes. First, the ideas represent their external causes, and secondly they resemble them. Reid does not like this move. If the direct object of knowledge is an idea, and the external object is never more than an indirect object of knowledge, it follows that we are never in a position to test the hypothesis that an idea resembles its external cause. To test it, after all, we should require equally direct access to both the external object and the internal one.

We might instead invoke the principle, already present in Plato's theory of forms and in Aristotle's theory of causation, that an effect is always a likeness, more or less, of its cause, much as the object which a fire heats resembles, in respect of heat, the fire which causes the heat. But invoking that principle could not be expected to impress Reid who would say that it was a piece of dogma, and was precisely what had first to be proved if we were to allow holders of the theory of ideas to argue that ideas resemble their external causes.

However, the chief issue here concerns not the qualities but the existence of the external causes of our ideas. If we reject the claim that in virtue of the resemblance relation between a cause and its effect we can discover the qualities of the external causes of our ideas by a consideration of the qualities of the ideas themselves, what we seem left with is this: that though there is an external cause of certain of our ideas we can know nothing about the cause except the fact of its existence. But we appear to have no entitlement to say even that much in the absence of any means of establishing direct contact with that cause. We should not lose sight of the possibility that the cause of an idea might be another idea. For Reid, the outcome of this line of enquiry is the rejection of the doctrine that ideas are the direct objects of knowledge, intermediate between our minds and external, indirectly known objects.

Reid grants that there is one virtue in this last mentioned position, a position he attributes to Hume. It is that it does at least follow from its premiss. Given that only an idea can be the immediate object of knowledge, the conclusion that we can have no knowledge whatever of external objects does seem to follow. However, Reid rejects the premiss that only an idea can be an immediate object of knowledge. He returns instead to his initial insight, that to have an idea of a given object X does not involve three elements, namely (1) an operation of the mind which operates directly on something, (2) the idea of X which is what the mind operates on directly, and (3) object X which the idea is an idea of. Instead having an idea involves two elements, an operation of the mind and an object X to which the mind is directed.

As regards criticism of Locke's version of the theory of ideas, there is one point on which Hume and Reid are in agreement, though I think neither philosopher mentions this fact. Whereas Locke accepts the foregoing list of three elements, Hume and Reid agree that the three elements are one too many. They do however disagree concerning which element should be deleted. Hume, according to Reid, rejects the third, whereas Reid rejects the second.

Reid traces the theory of ideas back to Greek philosophy. He finds clear sign of the theory in Plato and Aristotle, observes that it runs through Scholastic philosophy, and that it culminates in Hume's *Treatise*. Reid's position on this historical matter is plainly stated: 'all philosophers from Plato to Mr Hume, agree in this, That we do not perceive external objects immediately, and that the immediate object of perception must be some image present to the mind'.[127] This sentence is no throwaway remark. For Reid it lies at the heart of things. I wish here, however, to question the accuracy of the historical claim that it makes.

In Chapter 4 I offered an account of the medieval philosophical concept of a notion and focused upon the work done on that concept by members of the circle of John Mair. Here I shall argue that the role of notions in Mair's philosophy is the same as the role of ideas in Reid's. (1) Just as Mair regards notions as operations of the mind [*actus intelligendi*: acts of thought] so also does Reid regard ideas. (2) Just as Mair leaves no room for an object of knowledge intermediate between the notion of X and the external object X, so also Reid leaves no room for an object of knowledge intermediate between an idea, considered as a mental operation, and the object of which the idea is an idea. Certainly Mair affirmed that there are reflexive notions, that is, notions of notions, for he knew that we can reflect upon the operations of our mind. But this is not a matter on which Mair and Reid disagree, for Reid also accepted that we can have an idea of an idea. Such ideas occur when we reflect upon operations of the mind, thinking, remembering, conceiving, perceiving, and so on. It should perhaps be added that the existence of reflexive notions and of ideas of ideas does not have sceptical implications for the possibility of knowledge of the external world so long as it is allowed, as it was by Mair and Reid, that a reflexive notion is not possible, and neither is an idea of an idea, unless we can also have a notion which is not of another notion, and an idea which is not of another idea. But both Mair and Reid allowed that no notion or idea of an act of perception is possible unless we can have a notion or idea of an external object. Thus, consonant with (1) and (2) we can add (3) that just as Mair is not at all sceptical about the existence of external objects, neither is Reid. As a footnote to this comparison, it is interesting to recall a brief passage by Reid which I quoted earlier: 'To think of a thing, and to have a thought of it . . . to conceive a thing, and to have a conception, *notion, or idea* of it, are phrases perfectly synonymous' (my italics).

As shown in Chapter 4, Mair's theory of notions commits him to what may be termed a representative theory of perception. But I pointed out that the justification for the title is that notions are said to be representatives of what they are notions of. They are representative in so far as they have the same form as their objects and are directed to those objects. On this account Mair does not have a representative theory of perception if by that phrase is meant a theory such as Locke's, which treats ideas as immediate objects of knowledge which represent objects external to the mind.

It should be added that neither does Hume have a representative theory of perception in that sense of the phrase, but not at all for the reason that Mair does not. The reason Hume's theory is not a representative theory of perception in Locke's sense, is that Hume did not think that there was anything outside the mind for the ideas in the mind to represent. I do not wish to say baldly that Hume thought that there is nothing outside the mind, though it could be argued that he is committed to that view. I am saying only that our ideas are not representative of things outside, or of anything; our world is a world of ideas. We are here faced with Hume's so-called scepticism. It was because the theory of ideas led to Humean scepticism that Reid thought it necessary to refute the theory of ideas and to set up in opposition to it his own theory of Common Sense. That Reid thought there was indeed an opposition between himself and Hume on this matter is not in doubt, but I wish here to raise a question concerning what precisely the dispute was between the two men. We shall find it surprisingly difficult to answer that question.

Reid asserts that there is an external world, that there are causal relations between things, that his mental acts and operations are his, and that he has an immediate awareness of himself – for all his criticism of Descartes' application of the theory of ideas, Reid did not let go of Descartes' insight that doubt what he might, he cannot, while doubting, doubt also his own existence. We must ask whether Hume denies the existence of the external world, of causal necessity, and of himself. I think that the answer is that he does not. To take the first of these three, Hume ate meals, wrote books, served as a diplomat in Paris, and was the life and soul of several clubs in Edinburgh. This is not what we should expect of a person who did not believe in the existence of the external world. It is clear that Hume believed in it just as much as did Reid. What, then, is the dispute between the two? Reid says that its existence is a principle of common sense, in that its existence is not in need of, and does not admit of direct proof; it is however used as a premiss in all our scientific study of the world. Hume does not deny that we believe in the external world. But he is interested in determining the nature of the relationship between that world and ourselves who perceive it and act upon it. His answer is that there is no rational basis for the belief that the external world has a truly independent existence. He examines reasons for thinking that there is such a rational basis and he rejects them but there does after all seem to be a world external to, and therefore independent of, us, which we confront whenever we employ our sensory receptors. Can we account for the existence of this world? Reid says that we have a natural and irresistible belief in its existence.

For Hume, however, Reid's position, though true, does not address the question of what the existential status of the world is. In hardly-to-be-surpassed philosophy Hume gives an account of that status in terms of acts of mind, specifically acts of the faculty of imagination working upon present impressions and ideas. By means of those acts we construct for ourselves the world we think of as external to us, a world which presents itself to us as having an existence independent of us and our acts, whereas it is maintained in existence by an activity of imagination which is ceaseless during our waking hours. Of course we are not conscious of this constructive activity, and even to know about it, as Hume did, in a discursive rather than an intuitive way, does nothing whatever to shake belief in the existence of the independence of the world. That, for Hume, is the existential status of our world – it is an artifact produced and sustained by our imagination.

This is not to deny that what we call the external world really exists. On the contrary, Hume starts, as we all must, no doubt for reasons Reid articulated, by believing that the external world exists. The question for Hume was not a practical question concerning whether he will have certain experiences if he opens his eyes, or touches a hard surface. It is a theoretical one concerning our relation to it.

Much the same story can be told about Hume's account of the necessary connection between cause and effect. Hume is no more immune than any of us to the belief that the connection between a cause and its effect is a necessary one. Reid believes in the necessity and Hume does not deny it. What Hume does not know, and wishes to determine, is the nature of that necessity. He gives an answer in terms of the activity of the faculty of the imagination. If we have often seen one billiard ball collide with a second and each time have seen the second immediately start to move, next time we see a billiard ball collide with a second we form an idea of the second ball moving. This idea, a product of an act of imagination, is sufficiently lively to count, in Hume's terms, as a belief that the second billiard ball is about to move. In the light of our experience of observed constant conjunctions of events, say, of collision and subsequent movement, we thus form an expectation of an event of the second kind when we perceive an event of the first. Hume denies that he has an impression of necessary connection, and is led to ask whether we can therefore be said to have an idea of it either. But his procedure is misleading. How does he know that no impression he has is an impression of necessary connection unless he knows what he is looking for when he looks for such an impression? And how can he know what he is looking for unless he has an idea of it? And how is he able to tell us at the end of his search that what we call necessary connection is really a given expectation we have that is formed in the light of experience? The answer is, I think, that Hume does have an idea of necessary connection, but he believes that it has an existential status which is quite other than we might suppose it to be. The necessary connection between a cause and its effect does not exist independently of us, the perceivers, who see things as causally related. On the contrary, the necessary connection is a product of our own imagination, though imagination has a cunning which enables it so to project the necessary connection as to leave us with the irresistible belief that it is independent of us, the projectors.

Hume is therefore making the same basic move in respect of our belief in the necessity of the causal connection and in respect of our belief in the existence of the external world. The existence of necessity and of externality are not a matter of dispute between Hume and Reid. But Hume answers the metaphysical question concerning the existential status of necessity and externality, in such a way that he convinces Reid that he, Hume, does deny that there are such things as necessity and externality.

I conclude that there is a difference between Hume and Reid, and it lies in their analysis of the metaphysical status of things in whose existence we have a natural and irresistible belief. The difference is this: Hume accords to imagination a crucial role in the construction and maintenance of our world, a role which ensures that the world is in large measure a product of imagination. Reid accords no such role to the imagination or to any other of our psychological faculties. He says that he believes the world to be thus and so, and that though he cannot give a philosophical explanation of the fact that this is how the world is, that fact does not in the least diminish his conviction that that is how the world is. Hume says that he believes the world to be thus and so, that he can give a philosophical explanation of the fact that this is how the world is, and that his ability to give that account has no effect whatever on the strength of his conviction that that is how the world is. Consequently, Hume, faced with the full list of Reid's principles of common sense, would say 'yes' to all of them. The philosophy starts after that.

It is plausible to maintain that for Reid, on the other hand, not philosophy but theology starts thereafter. Reid, a son of the manse and a minister of the Kirk for many years, was a theologian whose theology emerges on almost every page of the *Essays on the Intellectual Powers*. Reid appears to have held that the truth of common sense beliefs is underpinned by a benevolent God who created us with such a nature as to find those beliefs irresistible. Such a God would not give us an irresistible belief in falsehoods. It is difficult to imagine a doctrine further removed from Hume's.[128]

10   Hume on Belief and Will

In my examination of philosophy in Pre-Reformation Scotland I attended to the writings of John Ireland and William Manderston on the subject of human freedom. I should like to end my examination of the Enlightenment by returning to that same subject, this time paying particular attention to David Hume. However, the theories of those earlier philosophers will duly resurface in the course of the discussion.

I shall be concerned with the question of the relation between belief and the will. That they are related is not in dispute. Most obviously, and uncontroversially, beliefs play a role as antecedents to acts of the will, to what we earlier termed 'elicited acts' [*actus eliciti*], for it is in the light of our beliefs, as well as of other things, that our acts of will have the content they have. It is because I believe I might otherwise get wet that I will to take my umbrella. Beliefs are also, and again uncontroversially, related to the will in that we cannot will something without believing that what we *will* will *be*. If I am in doubt as to whether I can bring about a given state of affairs, I cannot will to bring it about; I can at best try to bring it about or perhaps will to try to.

As regards the foregoing two kinds of relation between belief and will, the belief is antecedent to the act of will. Let us ask now whether the act of will can be antecedent to belief. I am not asking whether beliefs can be formed in the light of what we have willed; that question is too easily answered to be worth attention. Instead the question at issue is whether belief is subject to will, in the sense that we can will to believe. Whatever answer is given, inferences could be drawn which take us to the heart of crucial areas in theology and have a direct bearing on the salvation of souls. We have already observed, in Chapter 6, that just as medieval theologians disputed most other things so also disputes on this question duly occurred. Hume, of course, wrote the *Treatise* and the *Enquiry concerning the Human Understanding* as a philosopher and not in the least as a theologian but his discussion led him to the same conclusion as that held by Robert Holkot, one of the great medieval theologians, and a theologian who was at that point writing as a theologian and not as a philosopher. I shall start by considering Hume's position, and since without an understanding of Hume's teachings on the nature of will and of belief it is not possible to appreciate the strengths and weaknesses of his answer to the question of whether belief can be subject to will, I shall here make certain points about the concepts at issue.

Hume says of 'will' that ' 'tis impossible to define'. Yet that well known remark is preceded by this equally well known one: 'by the *will*, I mean nothing but *the internal impression we feel and are conscious of, when we knowingly give rise to any new motion of our body, or new perception of our mind*'.[129] On the face of it this is a definition, for 'an internal impression . . . ' is what Hume says he *means* by 'will'. If this is not a definition that he has given us then what is it? A likely answer is that it is a means of identification. It is possible to describe something in such a way as to enable others to pick out what is being referred to, without at the same time defining the term used, as when I say of my fountain pen that it is the black object lying on my desk, or when I say of a particular greeting that it is the form of words that a certain friend always uses. So perhaps Hume is not defining 'will', but is instead enabling us to pick out what he means by 'will' by telling us what the customary context of willing is.

It might however seem that Hume is giving a definition since in speaking of will as an internal impression he appears to be employing the classical method of defining *per genus et differentiam*, that is, stating what the general category [the *genus*] is to which the thing belongs and adding what it is about the thing that differentiates it [the *differentia*] from other things belonging to that same general category. However we have to respect the fact that Hume declares 'will' to be indefinable. It is probable that he has in mind a concept of definition according to which defining involves naming the elements of which a complex thing is composed and stating the relations between those elements, and since he believes will to be a simple impression the process of analysis essential to definition cannot occur.

Let us say, therefore, that Hume's seeming definition is not an attempt to define the term but is instead an attempt to inform us how to pick out an impression of will if such an impression should present itself to us. In that case it has to be said that his non-definition of 'will' is less informative than it should be. For in seeking an impression we are conscious of when we knowingly give rise to a new motion or perception, are we to look for something antecedent to the motion or perception, or something subsequent, or something concurrent? Hume's brief sentence does not tell us. Nevertheless it is plain from other texts that he has in mind an impression antecedent to the motion of the body or perception of the mind to which we knowingly give rise. Indeed it is plain from those texts, to which I shall shortly be turning, that in Hume's view the role of the will is to cause those motions and perceptions already referred to.

Since Hume's initial account of 'will' informs us that will is an internal impression (as opposed to an impression of sensation), and since he had previously spoken of a number of internal impressions, namely, the passions of pride and humility, love and hate, and desire, why did he not identify will with one or other of those impressions? He might have been expected to, for he thought of will as a cause of action, and it is plain that the passions and desire can readily be cast in that role.

Of the various internal impressions Hume discusses, the one with which will can most plausibly be identified is desire. But

Hume knew as well as anyone could that, however closely related will and desire were, and he knew them to be very closely related indeed, it would be wrong simply to identify one with the other. An important consideration here is that it is possible for a person to have two mutually conflicting desires, but he cannot have two volitions, that is, perform two acts of will, which are in mutual conflict. Also a person can desire to perform a given act though believing that he cannot now perform it, and perhaps believing that neither would he ever be able to. But he cannot will to perform it while believing that he might not be able to perform it. If, on the other hand, it is held that will is to be identified with any one of the passions Hume lists, such as pride or love, then it can be said in reply that while Hume believed will to be an impression we feel and are conscious of when we knowingly give rise to a motion or perception, it is obviously not true, as regards any one of the passions, that we feel and are conscious of it when we knowingly give rise to a motion or perception. For example, we do not always feel pride when we knowingly give rise to a motion or perception. Likewise with every other passion.

Thus, though Hume thinks will is like the passions and desire in that all these items are internal impressions and are related in some way to action, he does not think that will can be expounded in terms of passions and desire. Any attempt to identify will with a single passion or with desire fails at the hurdles just enumerated, and any attempt to identify will with several passions and desire in some given relation to each other fails to satisfy Hume's criterion of simplicity; for the will is, after all, a simple impression.

Far from suggesting an identification of will with a passion, it appears to be Hume's view that will plays a role as intermediary between the passions and action. In a famous passage Hume declares that reason is the slave of the passions. The dramatic phrase points to the doctrine that reason is 'inert' in so far as it can 'never oppose passion in the direction of [i.e. in giving directions to] the will'.[130] The implication of this is that the passions cause action through their influence upon the will. According to this interpretation of Hume, a characteristic human action can be identified by its place in a causal chain. Such an action is caused by an act of will (an internal impression) which is caused by a passion (another, and different kind of, internal impression). It is a different kind of internal impression, because an act of will is the kind of internal impression which can immediately cause an action, whereas a passion can cause an action mediately only, by causing an act of will which in turn causes an action of the kind which the passion would cause immediately if it could. If this is correct it follows that even though Hume does not offer an account of will in terms of other phenomena, he does offer just such an account of human action. A human action is a motion or perception which is the third and last item in the chain of causation whose first link is a passion and whose second is an act of will.

I should like now to raise a question concerning the kinds of phenomena which can occupy that third and last place in the causal chain. This question will lead to a better understanding of will. Since we cannot clarify the concept of will by saying what the elements of will are (for it is simple), perhaps we can learn something more about it by saying what sorts of thing it causes, and here we should remember that in seeking, in his non-definition, to shed light on will Hume refers to its causal power. Our attention will now be focused on that power.

We are told that the will can cause motions of the body and perceptions of the mind. But of course there is no suggestion that every possible motion of the body or perception of the mind is, or can be, subject to will. What is thus subject is discoverable only by experience, for the causality of the will is no different, according to Hume, from the causality of anything else in the world.[131] We discover a causal connection solely by observing constant conjunctions, and though, as we saw in the previous chapter, Hume did in a sense allow that there is such a thing as a necessary connection between a cause and its effect, the necessary connection is not an objective feature of the relation between cause and effect but an interpretation we place upon the observed relation. We, so to say, read a necessary connection into the relation. As observers looking for a causal connection we do not search for an impression of necessary connection. We search only for constant conjunctions; necessary connections can take care of themselves.

Hence in order to discover what the will causes we observe events with which an act of will is constantly conjoined and to which the act is temporally immediately antecedent. Only by such means do we discover that movements of limbs and head are subject to will but dilation of the pupils is not. There is absolutely no question that we have a privileged access into the power of will as a result of which we can determine, merely by a consideration of that faculty, in isolation from its effects, that it can produce certain things and not others. This most important feature of the will has an immediate bearing on the assessment we should make of Hume's teachings on the will in relation to Manderston's teaching on the same subject.

By observing constant conjunctions we can for example discover that much that goes on in our minds is subject to will: 'by an act or command of our will, we raise up a new idea, fix the mind to the contemplation of it, turn it on all sides, and at last dismiss it for some other idea . . . '[132] 'The mind has the command over all its ideas, and can separate, unite, mix, and vary them, as it pleases.'[133] But other things in the mind are not subject to will. Hume speaks of a certain sentiment or feeling which does not depend on will nor can be commanded at pleasure but instead, like all other sentiments, must be excited by nature.[134] It is possible that Hume is making the same point when he asserts: 'But 'tis certain we can naturally no more change our own sentiments, than the motions of the heavens.'[135]

Our lack of voluntary control over our affective life has immediate implications for the question of whether we have voluntary control over our beliefs, given the Humean account of the nature of belief. In discussing the difference between fiction and belief, Hume asserts that it 'lies in some sentiment or feeling, which is annexed to the latter, not to the former, and which depends not on the will . . . '[136] Likewise in his discussion of the conception which we have of a thing present to the senses or to the memory, and which is an element in belief, Hume asserts that 'this conception is attended with a feeling or sentiment, different from the loose reveries of the fancy'.[137] He adds that, whatever we believe, we can form a conception of the contrary of it, and that 'there would be no difference between the conception assented to and that which is rejected, were it not for some sentiment which distinguishes the one from the other'.[138] We should therefore expect Hume to hold that belief itself is not subject to will, and it can come as no surprise that he asserts: 'belief consists merely in a certain feeling or sentiment; in something, that depends not on the will, but must arise from certain determinate causes and principles, of which we are not masters'.[139] For example, since by an act or command of my will I can raise up a new idea, I can, while looking at this book-free table, raise up an idea of a book lying on the table. But though it can bring that idea into existence it is not within the power of my will that I should come to believe that there is a book on the table.

There is therefore good reason to suppose that for Hume the occurrence of any belief is to be explained by natural necessity and not by will. Where we cannot withhold assent, there we believe. If we can withhold it, then we are perhaps entertaining a concept but we are not believing. In the light of this characterisation of belief it has to be concluded that, for Hume, to believe is to give what the Pre-Reformation philosophers termed 'evident assent'. Inevident assent, as requiring an act of will, was simply not to count as belief.

This is not to say that Hume did not allow that the will can have an effect on belief. As we have noted, he speaks several times of the power of the will in the direction of the mind. If our attention is subject to will, as Hume plainly thinks it is, then the possibility has to be accepted that by directing our attention to some particular object we can come to believe something that we would not otherwise have believed.

An important Pre-Reformation distinction can usefully be employed here. Manderston speaks about two uses of the will, an applicative and an effective use.[140] By an act of will the agent heats water by applying fire to it. In such a case there is an element of freedom and an element of natural necessity, for the agent freely applies fire to the water but by natural necessity the fire heats the water. Here by an applicative act the will produces the heat of the water. The will is used effectively, by contrast, if by itself and without natural necessity playing a role the will secures its effect. The will can be used effectively to bring the intellect to bear upon evidences which naturally cause belief, and as a result of such an act of will I might, say, come to believe that a book is lying before me. This is compatible with Holkot's thesis, that belief is by natural necessity. For once I attend by an act of will to the table top, I cannot not believe that the book is on it. Thus though in this case I do not believe by the effective employment of my will, I do believe by the applicative employment of it, for it was only by an act of will that I attended to the table. Without that act I would not have had the belief. In that sense the belief is willed. As we saw, Manderston also held that some beliefs are held by an effective employment of the will.

From the foregoing discussion of Hume it is plain that he is committed to the view that we can come to believe by an applicative act of will, but not by an effective act. In that case Hume's position is in full accord with, and indeed is hardly distinguishable from, the first thesis of Robert Holkot's Commentary on the *Sentences of Peter Lombard*. Of course it follows that if Manderston's criticism of Holkot's thesis undermines that thesis it must also be effective against Hume's teaching on the relation between will and belief.

Fundamental matters are at issue here, for Hume's doctrine that belief is not subject to will is not an ad hoc element in his system, whose removal would leave that system otherwise intact. On the contrary, that doctrine is systematically related to a great deal of Hume's philosophy. Of course it has to be remembered that Manderston's own doctrine that some beliefs are subject to will is also deeply imbedded in his system. It is for example systematically related to his theological view that some beliefs are meritorious, and that we must therefore be accountable for them. Obviously he could not be expected lightly to surrender his position on the relation between belief and will. Too much is at stake.

I think that one response Manderston might give to Hume derives from Hume's teaching on the empirical basis of our discoveries of the power of the will. Hume is crystal clear in his discussion of whether will is on an equal footing with other causal agencies in respect of our inability to determine a priori what effects they might have in any given situation. Thus in speaking about the influence of volition over the organs of the body, he asserts that its influence 'is a fact, which, like all other natural events, can be known only by experience, and can never be foreseen from any apparent energy or power in the cause, which connects it with the effect, and renders the one an absolutely infallible consequence of the other'.[141] It is therefore by experience alone that we learn that our tongue and fingers are subject to our will and that our heart and liver are not. The question for Hume is therefore whether there is an observed constant conjunction between will and belief. He answers that there is not, and he could issue an ironic challenge to anyone to produce evidence to the contrary.

Hume's evidence is empirical and prompts the question

whether his report of a lack of constant conjunction is correct. In particular, Manderston could be expected to take up Hume's challenge, and say that it is his experience that belief is subject to will, or at any rate that beliefs of a certain kind are thus subject. At this point he can draw Hume's attention to the distinction between evident and inevident assent and claim that that to which we give inevident assent is not the less believed than is that to which we give evident assent. If Hume refuses to use the term 'belief' of the cases where inevident assent is given then that refusal, from Manderston's point of view, is based on an unjustified piece of verbal legislation. Hume could reply that where inevident assent is given, as for example when we decide to take someone's word on trust, and not just act as though we believe the person but actually believe him, then this is not in fact due to an act of will but is instead due to factors, psychological and perhaps also otherwise, which are suitable for investigation within the framework of an empirical scientific study of man.

It is evident that underlying the dispute about belief and will is a conflict between two radically different concepts of man. What would have to be considered therefore are the relative merits of those two concepts. In particular if Manderston's account of the relation between belief and will is correct then Hume's science of man requires revision. Whether Hume's account of the relation can after all withstand the criticism of it which is implicit in Manderston's writings, is a question it is not appropriate for me to address here. However, I hope I have shown that Manderston's position cannot lightly be dismissed, but on the contrary represents a serious challenge to the science of man that Hume sought to construct.

11 Conclusion

I have been focusing on two short periods in the history of Scottish philosophy, the first lasting for some three decades at the start of the sixteenth century, and the second lasting for the greater part of the eighteenth. The second began not quite two centuries after the first ended, and during that interim period the European philosophical scene in some respects changed almost beyond recognition. The greatest contributors to the change were the Protestant Reformation and renaissance humanism; but there were other more specific changes, which left a profound stamp upon the Enlightenment, and were almost certainly partial causes of it.

Two things can be mentioned here, first the Cartesian revolution in philosophy, which brought the theory of knowledge to the centre of the stage for the first time in the history of philosophy, and secondly the advent of Newtonian mechanics, seen by many as providing a model of explanation that philosophers had to adopt. As regards the first of these, the theory of ideas received its first clear, modern articulation in the writings of Descartes, and Hume investigated, more fully than any previous writer, the logical implications of that theory. It should be noted however that Hume did not raise any questions about the merits of the theory. He simply adopted it, without prior critical examination. In view of the fact that he was seeking to lay the foundations of a science of human nature it is surprising that Hume should be so uncritical about his starting point. In a sense it was precisely this fact which gave Thomas Reid his opening. He did subject the theory of ideas to close examination, and concluded that it was incoherent.

To turn briefly to the influence of Newtonian mechanics, these influenced Hume in several ways, in respect both of his philosophy and of the terminology he adopted. For example, we observed Hume speak of a uniting principle among ideas as 'a kind of ATTRACTION, which in the mental world will be found to have as extraordinary effects as in the natural, and to shew itself in as many and as various forms'.[142] For Hume, ideas gravitate to each other rather in the way that particles of matter do. The fact that Hume provides no mathematical formula of attraction of ideas corresponding to Newton's inverse square law does not count against his Newtonianism. It is commonly enough said that philosophy at any given time tends to employ the methods and concepts of the branch of science which is seen to be making the greatest progress, and Hume's Newtonianism is a conspicuous example of this association.

Remaining rather close to this commonplace, we should recall that Mair lived at the time of the discovery of America, a time when cartographers were literally having to redraw the map of the world. The discovery of America appealed to Mair as providing grounds for hope in other, non-physical, directions also. He wrote: 'Has not Amerigo Vespucci discovered lands unknown to Ptolemy, Pliny, and other geographers up to the present? Why cannot the same happen in other spheres?'[143] Likewise, and clearly according to the pattern of the relation between Newton and Hume, William Manderston's account of the nature of will was influenced by John Buridan's doctrine of impetus. We discussed Manderston's teaching on that matter in Chapter 6.

We have also dealt with specific similarities between the doctrines of Mair's circle and of the Scottish Enlightenment. I shall briefly mention two which are of particular significance. First, we observed that the theory of notions was based upon a certain conception of notions as acts or operations of the mind. Thus a perceptual notion is a mental act by which we apprehend a perceptual object. The act, so to say, reaches out into the physical world, enabling us to make immediate perceptual contact with it. A notion is therefore not to be thought of as an intermediate object between the knowing mind and the exernal object which is known. Consequently notions are to be contrasted with Cartesian or Lockean ideas, for such ideas are to be thought of as intermediate objects, through our knowledge of which we come to a knowledge of the external world. In line with this theory we observed Thomas Reid to hold that an idea is not what Descartes, Locke, or Hume thought it was, but is instead to be classified as an act or operation of the mind by which we gain unmediated knowledge of the world. Closer examination confirmed for us what this brief statement indicates, namely, that the concept of a notion, prevalent in Mair's circle, is to be identified with Reid's concept of an idea.

A second similarity concerns nominalism. We considered nominalism in connection with Lawrence of Lindores, and saw that it was the predominant stance of Mair and his associates. I attended particularly to the nominalist position concerning the doctrine of universals, but noted that their nominalism revealed itself at many points, for example, in their account of the nature of signification, for it was held that though we speak about the signification of a term, as though its signification is a quality inherent in the term, that is a metaphysical mistake. The signification is not literally in the term. If it is anywhere it is in us, and the fact that it appears to be in the term is due to our reading it into the term. Our philosophers spoke of 'imposition' of signification, in connection with their account of how a term comes to acquire a given signification in the first place. But in fact there is an important sense in which whenever we grasp the signification of a term we impose that signification upon it. To grasp the signification of the term is precisely to impose the signification upon it. Strictly speaking signification has the metaphysical status of an act of mind. This is a nominalist account.

Nominalism was strongly represented in the Scottish Enlightenment. In particular, Hume's philosophy is a continuation,
along nominalist lines, of the philosophy of some of his Pre-
Reformation predecessors. Indeed, from one point of view his
version of the theory of ideas ensured that he had to be
nominalist about almost everything. He recognised that realism
is the default position for us all: ' 'Tis certain, that almost all
mankind, and even philosophers themselves, for the greatest
part of their lives, take their perceptions to be their only objects,
and suppose, that the very being, which is intimately present to
the mind, is the real body or material existence.'[144] It was Reid,
more than anyone, who provided the philosophical under-
pinning for this 'default position'. Hume, however, believed the
position to be untenable and, given his theory of ideas, he could
not believe otherwise. His account of the mode of existence of
the external world is nominalist. As we observed, he argued that
what we call the 'external world' is largely, if not wholly, a
product of the acts of imagination by which we read externality
into our ideas – somewhat as we read signification into terms.
We create the world, and feel at home in it, and perhaps wonder
why, and the answer is that it is, in the fullest possible sense, our
world since we made it. It is made, a *fictum* or fiction, and it is
not surprising to find Hume using that word in the course of
his discussion. Speaking about the disparate perceptions out of
which we make the external world he refers to 'a propension to
unite these broken appearances by the fiction of a continu'd
existence . . . '[145]

Hume's nominalism is further represented in his account of
the mode of existence of the necessary connection between a
cause and its effect. He finds necessary connection not in the
cause or in the effect or in the relation between them, but in
a 'determination of the mind'. He writes: 'after a frequent
repetition, I find, that upon the appearance of one of the objects,
the mind is *determin'd* by custom to consider its usual attendant,

and to consider it in a stronger light upon account of its relation to the first object. 'Tis this impression, then, or *determination*, which affords me the idea of necessity.'[146] It is not that the necessary connection does not exist, but rather that it does not exist where we would expect to find it. We suppose, through what Reid would call our common sense, that the necessary connection is located where the cause and effect are. Hume located it in the perceiving subject, who sees a necessary connection in the causal relation because he has read the necessity into the relation. It is there, in so far as it is, because the perceiver has put it there, but metaphysically speaking the necessary connection is our way of understanding the world, rather than being a feature or element of the world.

There is a great deal that could be said about the relations between the philosophy of Mair's circle and the philosophy of the Scottish Enlightenment, and I have given only the briefest indication of some of those relations. A detailed study of the matter is not appropriate here. While it has been necessary to say something under that head, my chief concern has been to demonstrate that the mid-eighteenth century was not the only period when philosophy has flourished in Scotland. I have not sought to argue that, in respect of its philosophy, the Pre-Reformation period matches the Enlightenment, but the best that it had to offer amounts to an extraordinary philosophical achievement of Europe-wide significance. Those earlier philosophers had things to say which greatly interested their contemporaries, and which should interest us now, not merely because they are part of the history of the country, but because they shed light on problems of perennial concern. Work now being done on the ideas of the members on John Mair's circle is the best memorial that those philosophers could have.

Notes

1 Though this is the standard view, a radically different one is arguable. See A. Broadie, 'The rise (and fall?) of the Scottish Enlightenment', in T. M. Devine and J. Wormald (eds), *The Oxford Handbook of Scottish History* (Oxford, Oxford University Press, forthcoming 2012).

2 Edinburgh University, the fourth of Scotland's four 'ancient' universities, was founded in 1583, twenty-three years after the Reformation.

3 John Mair, *A History of Greater Britain as well England as Scotland*, p. 206.

4 For my interpretation of Scotus's philosophy and some indications of his influence on his successors, see my *The Shadow of Scotus*. I give a broad account in *A History of Scottish Philosophy*, pp. 7–33.

5 For details see Annie I. Dunlop (ed.), *Acta Facultatis Artium Universitatis Sanctiandree, 1413–1588* (Edinburgh, Scottish History Society, 1964).

6 For a nuanced view of Melville's role, see Steven J. Reid, *Humanism and Calvinism: Andrew Melville and the Universities of Scotland, 1560–1625* (Farnham, Ashgate, 2011).

7 Information on people who were responsible for the introduction of Hebrew into Scotland is to found in John Durkan, 'Native influences on George Buchanan', in *Acta Conventus Neo-Latini Sanctandreani: Proceedings of the Fifth International Congress of Neo-Latin Studies*, ed. I. D. McFarlane (Binghamton, Center for Medieval & Early Renaissance Studies, University Center at Binghamton, 1986); and John Durkan, 'George Hay's *Oration* at the purging of King's College, Aberdeen, in 1569: Commentary'.

8 J. H. Baxter, 'Four "new" mediaeval Scottish authors', *Scottish Historical Review* 25 (1928), pp. 90–7; and J. H. Baxter, 'The philosopher Laurence of Lindores', *Philosophical Quarterly*, 5 (1955), pp. 348–54. For additional information on his philosophy see: L. Moonan, 'Lawrence of Lindores (d. 1437) on Life in the Living Being' (PhD diss., University of Louvain, 1966).

9 Dunlop, *Acta Facultatis Artium*, 16 February 1418.

10 Ibid., 14 November 1438.

11 The two were James Resby, an English Wycliffist, and Pavel Kravar, a Hussite.

12 For further details see J. H. Burns, 'John Ireland and "The Meroure of Wyssdome" '; J. H. Burns, 'John Ireland: Theology and public affairs in the late fifteenth century', *Innes Revue* 41 (1990), pp. 151–81.

13 See Jean Crevier, *Histoire de l'Université de Paris* (Paris, 1761), vol. 4, pp. 363–5, 391–4.

14 John Ireland, *The Meroure of Wyssdome by Johannes de Irlandia*, vol. 2, p. 116.

15 Ibid., p. 117.

16 Ibid., p. 121.

17 Ibid., p. 132.

18 Ibid., p. 135.

19 Ibid., p. 137.

20 Ibid., p. 143.

21 For details see W. Beattie, 'Two notes on fifteenth-century printing: I. Jacobus Ledelh', *Edinburgh Bibliographical Society Transactions* 3 (1950), pp. 75–7.

22 See A. Broadie, 'James Liddell on concepts and signs', in A. A. Macdonald et al. (eds), *The Renaissance in Scotland* (Leiden, E. J. Brill, 1994), pp. 82–94.

23 Information on his life is to be found in A. Broadie, *George Lokert: Late Scholastic Logician*; A. Broadie, *The Circle of John Mair: Logic and Logicians in Pre-Reformation Scotland*; and A. Broadie, 'John Mair', *Oxford Dictionary of National Biography* (Oxford, Oxford University Press, 2004). See also J. H. Burns, 'The Scotland of John Major', and 'New light on John Major'. Also John Durkan, 'John Major: after 400 years', *Innes Review* 1 (1950), pp. 131–9, and 'The school of John Major: bibliography', *Innes Review* 1 (1950), pp. 140–57. Also Hubert Elie, 'Quelques maîtres de l'université de Paris vers l'an 1500', *Archives d'histoire doctrinale et littéraire du moyen âge* 25–6 (1950–1), pp. 193–243. Also James Farge, *Biographical Register of Paris Doctors of Theology 1500–1536*. Also Aeneas Mackay, 'Life of the author'. Also A. Ross, 'Some Scottish Catholic historians', *Innes Review* 1 (1950), pp. 5–21.

24 John Mair, *In primum Sententiarum*, fol. 34 *recto* col. 1.

25 Valuable bibliographical and doctrinal material is to be found in Vicente Muñoz Delgado, *Lógica Hispano-Portuguesa hasta 1600*.

26 J. Durkan and J. Kirk, *The University of Glasgow, 1451–1577* (Glasgow, University of Glasgow Press,1977).

27 John Knox, *John Knox's History of the Scottish Reformation*, ed. W. C. Dickinson, vol. 1, p. 15.

28 See Broadie, *George Lokert*, pp. 20–31; 'George Lokert', *Oxford Dictionary of National Biography*.

29 See Durkan and Kirk, *The University of Glasgow*, pp. 209.

30 Scottish Record Office, B13/10/1, Cupar Council Book, fol. 84 *recto*. See A. Broadie, 'William Manderston', *Oxford Dictionary of National Biography*.

31 See A. Broadie, *Introduction to Medieval Logic*, pp. 13–19.

32 George Lokert, *Termini*, fol. 22 *recto*.

33 Cf. David Cranston, *Terminorum*, sig. e3, in his *Sequunter abbreviationes omnium parvorum logicalium*.

34 John Mair, *Termini*, fol. 2 *recto* col. 2, in his *Libri quos in artibus regentando compilavit*.

35 David Cranston, *Tractatus noticiarum*, sig. b 1 *recto* col. 1.

36 Gilbert Crab, *Tractatus noticiarum*, sig. a 2 *recto* col. 1.

37 George Lokert, *Scriptum in materia noticiarum*, sig. a 2 *recto* col. 1.

38 Ibid., *sig.* c 4 *verso* col. 2

39 Mair, *Termini*, fol. 2 *recto* col. 2.

40 John Locke, *An Essay Concerning Human Understanding*, Bk I, ch. 1.

41 Lokert, *Scriptum in materia noticiarum*, *sig.* c 7 *recto* cols 1–2.

42 Mair, *In primum Sententiarum*, fol. 33 *recto* col. 2.

43 Lokert, *Scriptum in materia noticiarum*, *sig.* e 8 *recto* col. 1.

44 A. Broadie, *Notion and Object*, pp. 128–33.

45 Mair, *In primum Sententiarum*, fol. 6 *verso* col. 1.

46 Lokert, *Scriptum in materia noticiarum*, sig. e 8 *verso* cols 1–2

47 Ibid., col. 2.

48 Mair, *In primum Sententiarum*, fol. 1 *verso* col. 2.

49 Ibid.

50 Lokert, *Scriptum in materia noticiarum*, *sig.* f 5 *recto* cols 1–2.

51 Ibid., col. 2.

52 See A. Broadie, *The Shadow of Scotus*, ch. 6.

53 See E. K. Cameron, 'An early humanist edition of Aristotle at St Andrews', *The Bibliotheck* 9 (1978–9), pp. 65–71.

54 Knox, *John Knox's History*, pp. 219–29.

55 William Manderston, *Bipartitum in morali philosophia*.

56 Ibid., *sig.* d 2 *verso* col. 1.

57 Ibid., *sig.* c 5 *recto* col. 1.

58 Ibid., *sig.* b 1 *verso* col. 2.

59 For primary sources and discussion see Marshall Clagett, *The Science of Mechanics in the Middle Ages* (Madison, University of Wisconsin Press, 1959), pp. 505–40.
60 Manderston, *Bipartitum, sig.* b 3 *recto* col. 2; cf. sig. g 6 *verso* col. 2.
61 Ibid., sig. d 1 *verso* col. 1.
62 Ibid., sig. d 1 *recto* col. 2.
63 Ibid., *sig.* d 2 *recto* col. 2.
64 Ibid., *sig.* d 3 *recto* col. 1.
65 Ibid., *sig.* e 8 *recto* col. 2.
66 Ibid., *sig.* e 8 *verso* col. 1.
67 Ibid.
68 Ibid., *sig.* f 1 *verso* col. 1.
69 Ibid., *sig.* c 1 *verso* col. 2.
70 Ibid., *sig.* c 7 *recto* col. 2.
71 Ibid., *sig.* i 8 *recto* col. 2 – *verso* col. 1.
72 Ibid., *sig.* b 1 *verso* col. 1.
73 G. G. Smith (ed.), *The Poems of Robert Henryson*, 3 vols (Edinburgh, Scottish Text Society, 1906–14), vol. 3, p. 109, lines 17–20.
74 Ireland, *Meroure*, vol. 2, p. 131.
75 Manderston, *Bipartitum, sig.* k 1 *verso* col. 1.
76 Ibid., col. 2.
77 Ibid., col. 1.
78 Ibid., *sig.* k 1 *verso* col. 2 – *recto* col. 1.
79 Knox, *John Knox's History*, vol. 2, pp. 220–1.
80 A. Renaudet, *Préréforme et humanisme à Paris*, p .614.
81 Aristotle, *Nicomachean Ethics*, 1094 a 1–3.
82 Broadie, *Introduction to Medieval Logic*, pp. 114–17.
83 J. Durkan, 'Rutherford and Montaigne: An early influence'. There are also helpful references in I. D. McFarlane, *Buchanan*.
84 Steven Reid and Emma Wilson (eds), *Ramus, Pedagogy and the Liberal Arts: Ramism in Britain and the Wider World. A Collection of Essays on the French Educational Reformer Petrus Ramus, 1515–1572* (Farnham, Ashgate, forthcoming 2011),
85 See Durkan and Kirk, *The University of Glasgow* for references.
86 Numerous Scots at the universities of the Netherlands are mentioned in Paul Dibon, *L'enseignement philosophique dans les universités néerlandaises*.
87 *Commentarius R. Balforei in Organum Logicum Aristotelis* (Bordeaux, 1616); *R. Balforei Scoti Commentariorum in Lib. Arist. de Philosophia Tomus Secundus quo post organum logicum quaecumque in libris Ethicorum occurrunt difficilia dilucide explicantur* (Paris, 1620).

88 Florentius Volusenus, *Commentatio quaedam theologica*, p. 9.
89 Ibid., p. 31.
90 Ibid., p. 8.
91 Florentius Volusenus, *De anima tranquillitate dialogus* p. 19.
92 Ibid., p. 47.
93 Ibid., p. 48.
94 Ibid., p. 212.
95 There is invaluable material on this in J. Durkan, 'King Aristotle and Old "Butterdish": The making of a graduate in seventeenth-century Glasgow'. See also C. King, 'Newtonianism in Scottish universities in the seventeenth century', in R. H. Campbell and Andrew S. Skinner, *The Origins and Nature of the Scottish Enlightenment* (Edinburgh, John Donald, 1982), pp. 65–85.
96 A. Broadie, 'James Dundas and his concept of moral philosophy', in *The Journal of Scottish Thought* 2 (2009), pp. 99–112. The book is in neo-Latin. I am preparing an edition for publication.
97 C. M. Shepherd, 'Philosophy and science in the Arts curriculum of the Scottish universities in the seventeenth century' (PhD diss., University of Edinburgh, 1975).
98 For a brief account of Hutcheson's career see James Coutts, *A History of the University of Glasgow from its Foundation in 1451 to 1909*. See also the entry on Hutcheson in the *Oxford Dictionary of National Biography*.
99 Francis Hutcheson, *An Essay on the Nature and Conduct of the Passions and Affections*. This, and the following quotes, are from pp. 17–18.
100 David Hume, *Letters of David Hume*, ed. J. Y. T. Greig, vol. 1, letter 3, p. 13.
101 David Hume, *My Own Life*, in *Essays, Moral, Political and Literary*, ed. E. F. Miller, p. xxxiv.
102 Ibid., p. xxxvi.
103 Hume, *Letters*, vol. 2, p. 452.
104 David Hume, *A Treatise of Human Nature*, ed. L. A. Selby-Bigge, pp. 1–2
105 Ibid., p. 1.
106 Ibid., p. 3.
107 David Hume, *An Enquiry Concerning Human Understanding*, ed. L. A. Selby-Bigge, p. 21.
108 Ibid., p. 17.
109 Hume, *Treatise*, pp. 12–13.
110 Norman Kemp Smith, *The Philosophy of David Hume*.
111 See e.g. Hume, *Treatise*, p. 187.

112 Hume, *Enquiry*, p. 9.
113 Hume, *Treatise*, p. 252
114 For a brief biography of Reid see A. Broadie, 'Reid in context', in T. Cuneo and R. van Woudenberg (eds), *The Cambridge Companion to Thomas Reid*, pp. 31–52.
115 Immanuel Kant, *The Critique of Pure Reason*, trans. N. Kemp Smith (London, Macmillan, 1933), pp. 111–28.
116 M. Dummett, *Frege: Philosophy of Language*, 2nd edn (London, Duckworth, 1981), pp. 56–7
117 Thomas Reid, *Essays on the Intellectual Powers*, Essay I, ch. 1, p. 27.
118 Ibid., ch. 2, p. 39.
119 Ibid., p. 41.
120 Ibid., Essay VI, ch. 5, p. 470.
121 Ibid., Essay I, ch. 2, p. 42.
122 Ibid., Essay VI, ch. 5, p. 470.
123 Ibid., Essay I, ch. 2, p. 42.
124 Ibid., pp. 42–3.
125 Ibid., p. 44.
126 Ibid., Essay II, ch. 9, pp. 131–2.
127 Ibid., ch. 7, p. 105.
128 For a different account of the relation between Reid's theology and his common sense philosophy see D. F. Norton, *David Hume: Common-Sense Moralist, Sceptical Metaphysician*, pp. 200–5.
129 Hume, *Treatise*, p. 399.
130 Ibid., p. 413.
131 Hume, *Enquiry*, pp. 66, 68.
132 Ibid., p. 67.
133 Hume, *Treatise*, pp. 623–4.
134 Hume, *Enquiry*, p. 48.
135 Hume, *Treatise*, p. 517.
136 Hume, *Enquiry*, p. 48.
137 Ibid.
138 Ibid.
139 Hume, *Treatise*, p. 624.
140 Manderston, *Bipartitum sig.* e 8 *verso* col. 1.
141 Hume, *Enquiry*, pp. 64–5.
142 Hume, *Treatise*, pp. 12–13.
143 John Mair, *In quartum Sententiarum* (Paris, 1519), fol. 55.
144 Hume, *Treatise*, p. 206.
145 Ibid., p. 205.
146 Ibid., p. 156.

Bibliography

Allan, David, *Virtue, Learning and the Scottish Enlightenment* (Edinburgh, Edinburgh University Press, 1993)

Árdal, P. S., *Passion and Value in Hume's Treatise* (Edinburgh, Edinburgh University Press, 1966)

Broadie, A., *George Lokert: Late-Scholastic Logician* (Edinburgh, Edinburgh University Press, 1983)

Broadie, A., *The Circle of John Mair: Logic and Logicians in Pre-Reformation Scotland* (Oxford, Clarendon Press, 1985)

Broadie, A., *Notion and Object: Aspects of Late-Medieval Epistemology* (Oxford, Clarendon Press, 1989)

Broadie, A., *Introduction to Medieval Logic*, 2nd edn (Oxford, Clarendon Press, 1993)

Broadie, A., *The Shadow of Scotus: Philosophy and Faith in Pre-Reformation Scotland* (Edinburgh, T. & T. Clark, 1995)

Broadie, A., *The Scottish Enlightenment: The Historical Age of the Historical Nation* (Edinburgh, Birlinn, 2007)

Broadie, A., *A History of Scottish Philosophy* (Edinburgh, Edinburgh University Press, 2009)

Broadie, A. (ed.), *The Cambridge Companion to the Scottish Enlightenment* (Cambridge, Cambridge University Press, 2003)

Burns, J. H., 'The Scotland of John Major', *Innes Review* 2 (1951), pp. 65–76

Burns, J. H., 'New light on John Major', *Innes Review* 5 (1954), pp. 83–100

Burns, J. H., 'John Ireland and "The Meroure of Wyssdome" ', *Innes Review* 6 (1955), pp. 77–98

Coutts, James, *A History of the University of Glasgow from its Foundation in 1451 to 1909* (Glasgow, Glasgow University Press, 1909)

Crab, Gilbert, *Tractatus noticiarum* (Paris, c. 1503)

Cranston, David, *Terminorum,* in *Sequuntur abbreviationes omnium parvorum logicalium collecte a magistro Anthonio Ramirez de Villascusa cum aliquibus divisionibus terminorum eiusdem: necnon cum tractatu terminorum magistri Davidis Cranston ab eodem correcto* (Paris, c. 1513)

Cranston, David, *Tractatus noticiarum parvulis et provectis utilissimus* (Paris, 1517)

Cranston, William, *Dialecticae compendium* (Paris, 1540; 2nd edn Paris, 1545)

Cross, Richard, *Duns Scotus on God* (Aldershot, Ashgate, 2005)

Cross, Richard, *Duns Scotus* (Oxford, Oxford University Press, 2009)

Cuneo, Terence and René van Woudenberg (eds), *The Cambridge Companion to Thomas Reid* (Cambridge, Cambridge University Press, 2004)

Davidson, William, *Gulielmi Davidson Aberdonani institutiones inculentae iuxta ac breves in totum Aristotelis organum logicum* (Paris, 1560)

Davie, G. E., *The Democratic Intellect: Scotland and her Universities in the Nineteenth Century,* 2nd edn (Edinburgh, Edinburgh University Press, 1961)

Davie, G. E., *The Crisis of the Democratic Intellect:The Problem of Generalism and Specialism in Twentieth-Century Scotland* (Edinburgh, Polygon, 1986)

Dempster, John, *Dialogus de argumentatione* (Paris, 1554)

Dibon, Paul, *L'enseignement philosophique dans les universités néerlandaises à l'époque pré-cartésienne, 1575–1650* (Paris, Elsevier, 1954)

Durkan, John, 'John Rutherford and Montaigne: An early influence?', *Bibliothèque d'Humanisme et Renaissance* 41 (1979), pp. 115–22

Durkan, John, 'King Aristotle and Old "Butterdish": The making of a graduate in seventeenth-century Glasgow', *College Courant* 63 (1979), pp. 18–24

Durkan, John, 'George Hay's *Oration* at the purging of King's College, Aberdeen, in 1569: Commentary', *Northern Scotland* 6 (1984–5), pp. 97–112

Farge, James, *Biographical Register of Paris Doctors of Theology, 1500–1536* (Toronto, Pontifical Institute of Medieval Studies, 1980)

Galbraith, Robert, *Quadrupertitum in oppositiones conversiones hypotheticas et modales Magistri Roberti Caubraith* (Paris, 1510)

Hume, David, *The Letters of David Hume*, ed. J. Y. T. Greig, 2 vols (Oxford, Clarendon Press, 1932)

Hume, David, *Enquiries concerning Human Understanding and concerning the Principles of Morals*, ed. L. A. Selby-Bigge, 3rd edn, rev. P. H. Nidditch (Oxford, Clarendon Press, 1975)

Hume, David, *A Treatise of Human Nature*, ed. L. A. Selby-Bigge, 2nd edn, rev. P. H. Nidditch (Oxford, Clarendon Press, 1978)

Hume, David, *Essays Moral, Political and Literary*, ed. E. F. Miller, rev. edn (Indianapolis, Liberty Fund, 1985)

Hutcheson, Francis, *An Essay on the Nature and Conduct of the Passions and Affections with Illustrations on the Moral Sense* (London, 1728; reprint, ed. A. Garrett, Indianapolis, Liberty Fund, 2002)

Hutcheson, Francis, *A System of Moral Philosophy*, 2 vols (London, 1755; reprint, intr. Daniel Carey, London, Continuum, 2005)

Ireland, John, *The Meroure of Wyssdome by Johannes de Irlandia*, vol. 2, ed. J. F. Quinn (Edinburgh, Blackwood, 1965)

Kemp Smith, Norman, *The Philosophy of David Hume* (London, 1941; reprint, intr. D. Garrett, Basingstoke, Palgrave Macmillan, 2005)

Knox, John, *John Knox's History of the Reformation in Scotland*, ed. W. C. Dickinson, 2 vols (London, Nelson, 1949)

Liddell, James, *Tractatus conceptuum et signorum* (Paris, 1495)

Locke, John, *An Essay concerning Human Understanding*, ed. P. H. Nidditch (Oxford, Oxford University Press, 1975)

Lokert, George, *Scriptum in materia noticiarum* (Paris, 1514)

Lokert, George, *Termini* (Paris, *c.* 1523)

McFarlane, I. D., *Buchanan* (London, Duckworth, 1981)

Mackay, Aeneas J. G., 'Life of the author', printed as preface to John Mair's *A History of Greater Britain* . . . , trans. and ed. A. Constable (Edinburgh, Printed by T. and A. Constable for the Scottish History Society, 1892)

Mair, John, *Libri quos in artibus regentando compilavit*, ed. A. Coronel (Paris, 1506)

Mair, John, *In primum Sententiarum* (Paris, 1519)

Mair, John, *In secundum Sententiarum* (Paris, 1519)

Manderston, William, *Bipartitum in morali philosophia* (Paris, 1517)

Manderston, William, *Tripartitum epithoma doctrinale et compendiosum in totius dyalectices artis principia Guillelmo Manderston Scoto nuperrime collectum* (Paris, 1517)

Millican, Peter (ed.), *Reading Hume on Human Understanding: Essays on the First Enquiry* (Oxford, Clarendon Press, 2002)

Mossner, E. C., *The Life of David Hume*, 2nd edn (Oxford, Clarendon Press, 1970)

Muñoz Delgado, Vicente, *Lógica Hispano-Portuguesa hasta 1600 (Notas bibliográfico-doctrinales)* (Salamanca, [s.n.], 1972)

Norton, David Fate, *David Hume: Common-Sense Moralist, Sceptical Metaphysician* (Princeton, Princeton University Press, 1982)

Reid, Thomas, *An Inquiry into the Human Mind on the Principles of Common Sense*, eds Derek R. Brookes and Knud Haakonssen (Edinburgh, Edinburgh University Press, 1997)

Reid, Thomas, *Essays on the Intellectual Powers of Man*, eds Derek R. Brookes and Knud Haakonssen (Edinburgh, Edinburgh University Press, 2002)

Reid, Thomas, *Thomas Reid on Logic, Rhetoric and the Fine Arts*, ed. A. Broadie (Edinburgh, Edinburgh University Press, 2005)

Reid, Thomas, *Essays on the Active Powers of Man*, eds Knud Haakonssen and James A. Harris (Edinburgh, Edinburgh University Press, 2011)

Renaudet, A. *Préréforme et humanisme à Paris pendant les premières guerres d'Italie (1494–1517)*, 2nd edn (Paris, Librairie d'Argences, 1953)

Rutherford, John [Joannes Retorfortis] *Commentariorum de arte disserendi libri quatuor* (Edinburgh, 1557; 2nd edn Edinburgh, 1577)

Smith, Adam, *The Theory of Moral Sentiments*, eds D. D. Raphael and A. L. Macfie (Oxford, Clarendon Press, 1976; Indianapolis, Liberty Fund, 1982)

Stewart, M. A., 'John Smith and the Molesworth Circle', *Eighteenth-Century Ireland* 2 (1987), pp. 89–102

Tod, Patrick, *Dialecticae methodus* (Paris, 1544)

Volusenus, Florentius, *Commentatio quaedam theologica* (Lyons, 1539)

Volusenus, Florentius, *De animi tranquillitate dialogus* (Lyons, 1543)

Index